# RECORDED VERSIONS GUITAR

AUTHENTIC TRANSCRIPTIONS
WITH NOTES AND TABLATURE

# GUITAR TAB 2004

## 15 OF THE HOTTEST HITS!

W9-AVH-635

# CONTENTS

ISBN 0-634-08613-8

HAL•LEONARD®
CORPORATION
7777 W. BLUEMOUND RD. P.O. BOX 13819 MILWAUKEE, WI 53213

Visit Hal Leonard Online at
www.halleonard.com

# All Downhill From Here

### Words and Music by Cyrus Bolooki, Chad Gilbert, Jordan Pundik, Ian Grushka and Steve Klein

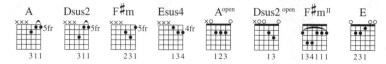

*Chord symbols reflect overall harmony.

**Verse**

1. You're hid - ing some - thing 'cause it's burn - ing through your eyes.

I try to get it out but all I hear from you are — lies.

**Pre-Chorus**

And I can tell you're go - ing through the mo - tions,

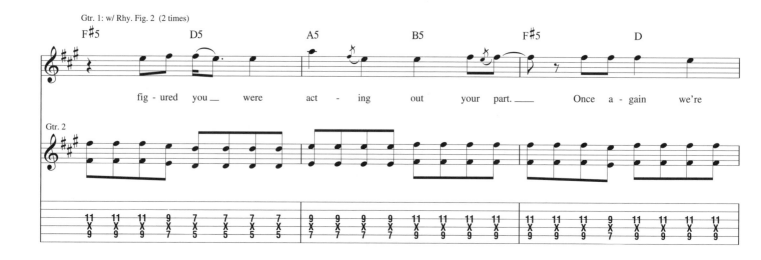

Gtr. 1: w/ Rhy. Fig. 2 (2 times)

fig - ured you __ were act - ing out your part. __ Once a - gain we're

play - ing off e - mo - tion. Which one of us will burn un - til the end? __

**Chorus**
**Half-time feel**

__ Cat - a - lyst, __ you in - sist to pull __ me down. __ You

*Composite arrangement

4

con-tra-dict___ the fact___ that you ___ still want me a-round.___ And it's___

all down-hill___ from here.___ And it's__

all down-hill___ from here.___

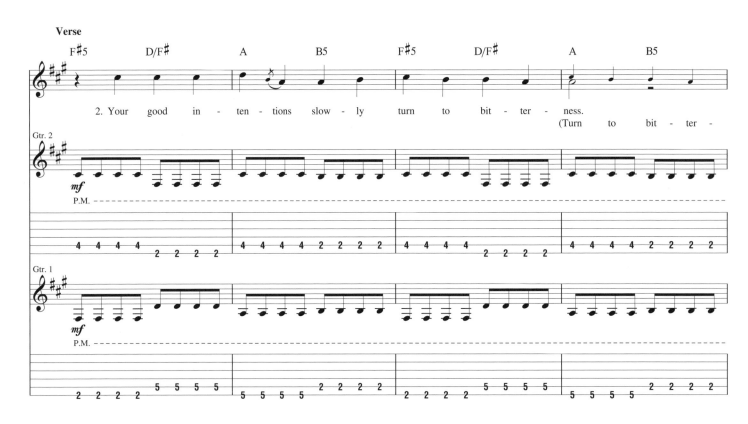

2. Your good in - ten - tions slow - ly turn to bit - ter - ness.
(Turn to bit - ter -

Re - oc - cur - ring ep - i - sodes with each and ev - 'ry kiss. _____
ness.) (Let's go!)

*D.S. al Coda*

**Pre-Chorus**

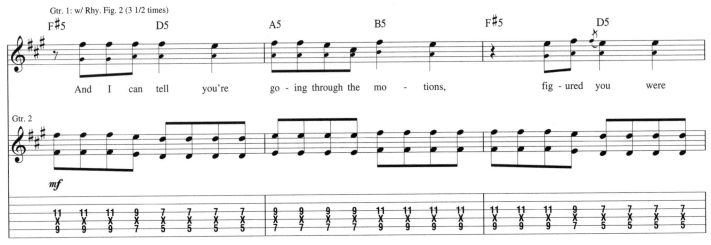

And I can tell you're go - ing through the mo - tions, fig - ured you were

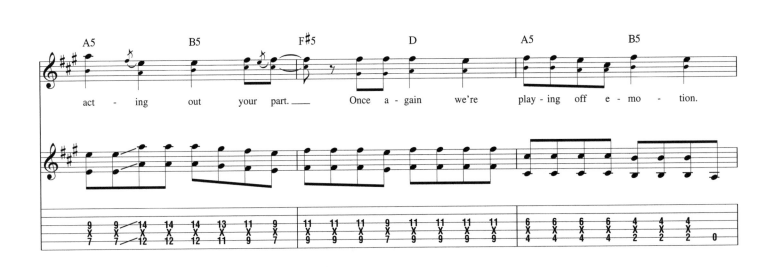

act - ing out your part. ___ Once a - gain we're play - ing off e - mo - tion.

**Chorus**

Which one of us will burn un - til the end? ___ Cat - a - lyst, ___

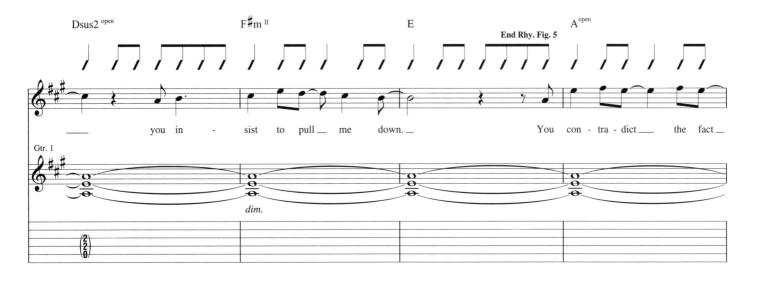

you in - sist to pull me down. ___ You con - tra - dict ___ the fact

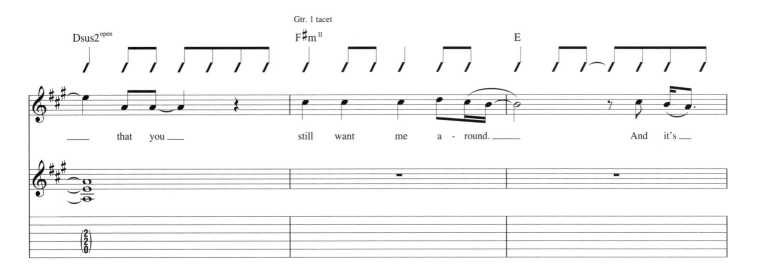

___ that you ___ still want me a - round. ___ And it's ___

all down - hill ___ from here. ___ And it's ___

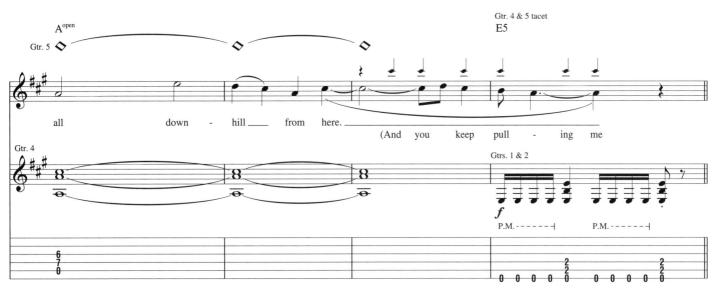

all down - hill ___ from here. ___

(And you keep pull - ing me

**Outro**

**Half-time feel**

Gtrs. 1 & 2: w/ Rhy. Fig. 3 (3 3/4 times)
Gtr. 3: w/ Rhy. Fig. 3A (3 3/4 times)

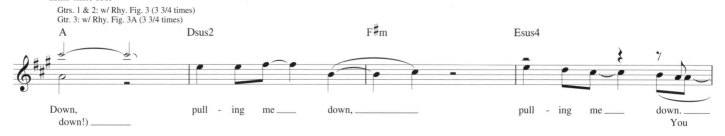

Down,     pull - ing me \_\_\_ down, _____ pull - ing me \_\_\_ down. \_\_\_\_
down!) \_\_\_       You

con - tra - dict \_\_\_ the fact \_\_\_ that you \_\_\_ still want me a - round. \_\_\_ And it's \_\_\_

Gtr. 4: w/ Riff A (1 3/4 times)

all    down - hill \_\_\_ from here. _____ And it's \_\_\_

**End half-time feel**

Gtrs. 1 & 2: w/ Rhy. Fig. 4 (2 times)
Gtr. 3: w/ Riff B (2 times)

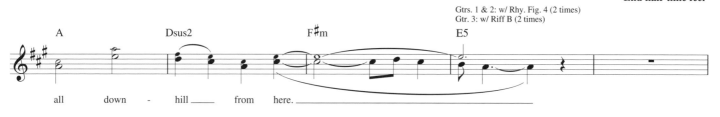

all    down - hill \_\_\_ from here. _____

# Cold Hard Bitch

**Words and Music by Nic Cester, Chris Cester and Cameron Muncey**

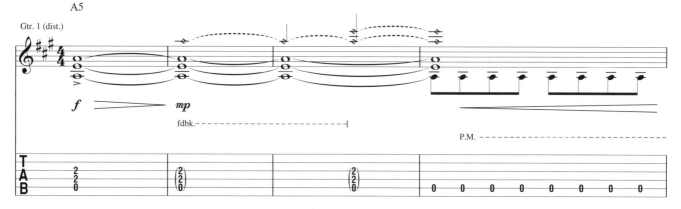

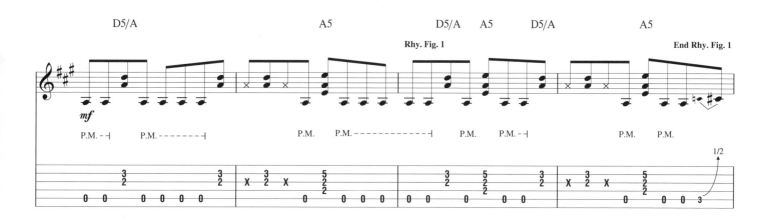

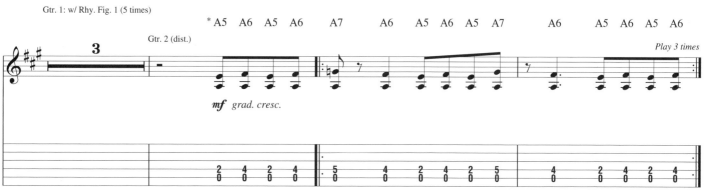

*Chord symbols refer to Gtr. 2 only.

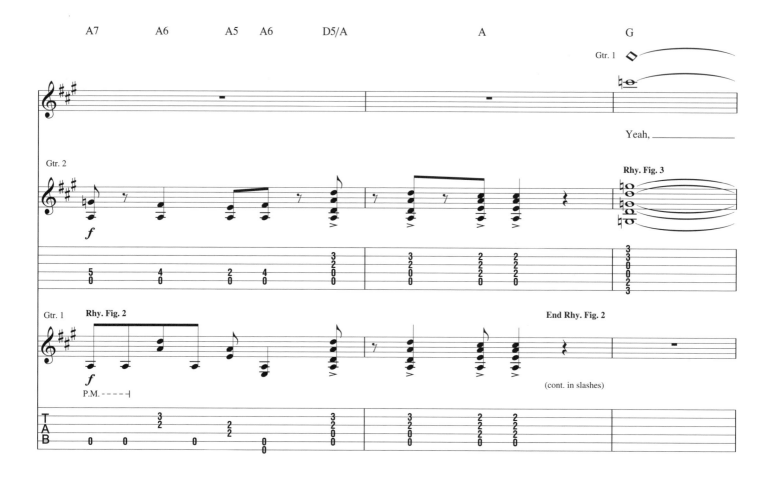

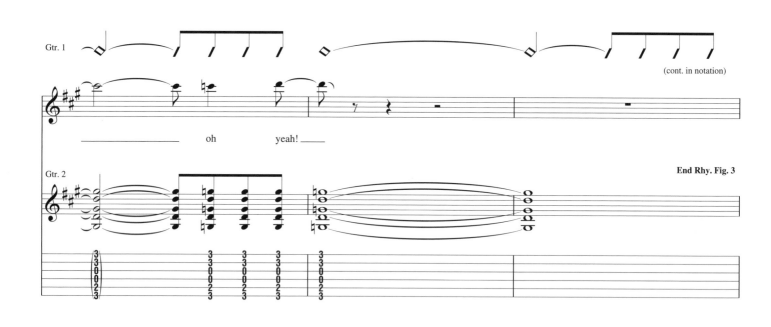

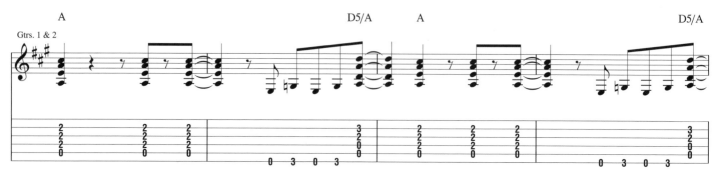

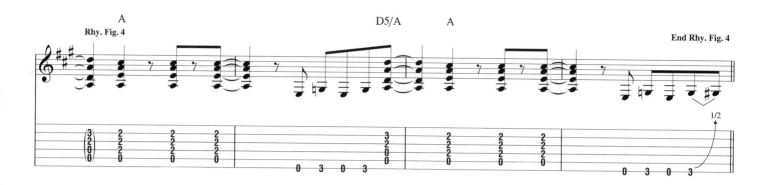

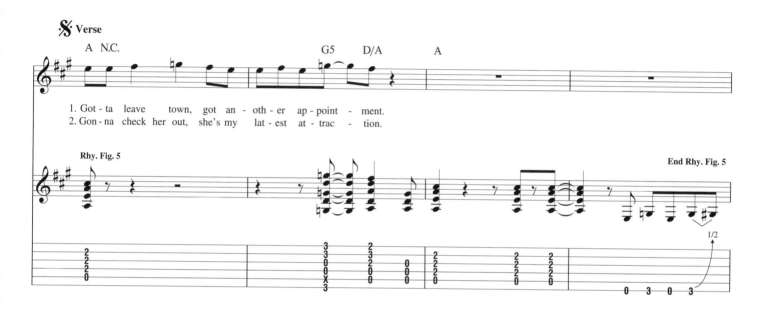

Cold hard bitch, __ she was shak-in' her hips, __ well, that was all that I need. __ I'm

wait-ing, give me. Cold hard bitch. __ Just a kiss on the lips __ and I was on my knees.

Yeah, __ I'm wait - ing. Yeah, __ I'm

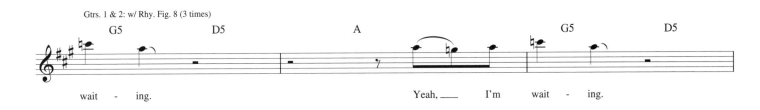

wait - ing. Yeah, _____ I'm wait - ing.

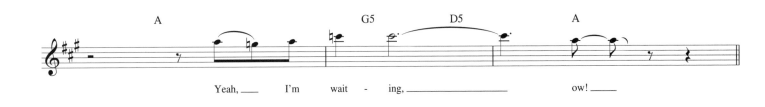

Yeah, _____ I'm wait - ing, _____ ow!

### Interlude

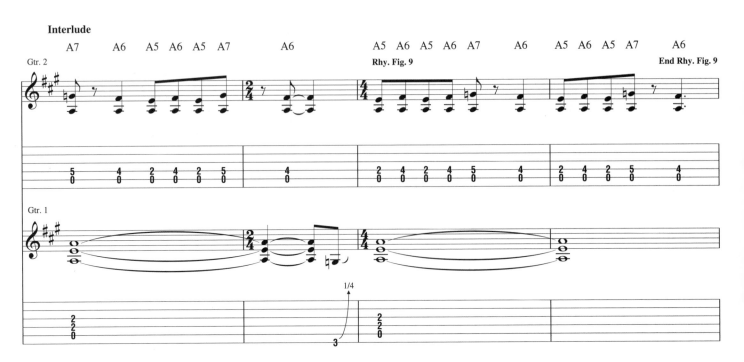

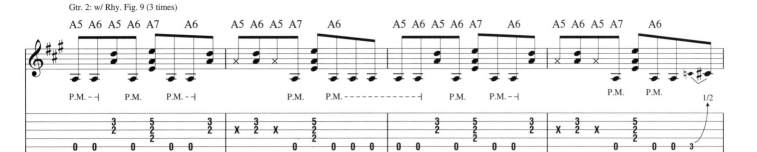

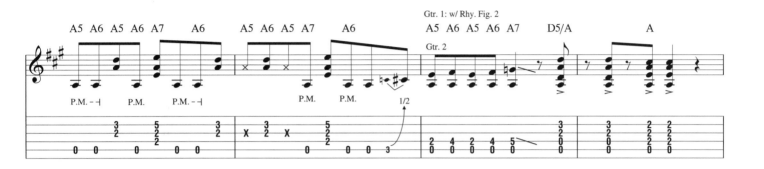

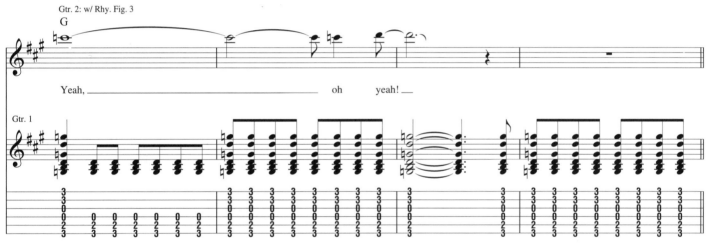

Yeah, _____ oh yeah! __

**Chorus**

Gtrs. 1 & 2: w/ Rhy. Fig. 6 (3 times)

Cold hard bitch. _ Just a kiss on the lips _ and I was on my knees. _ I'm wait - ing, give me.

Cold hard bitch, _ she was shak - in' her hips, _ well, that was all that I need. _ I'm wait - ing, give me.

Cold hard bitch. _ Just a kiss on the lips _ and I was on my knees. _ I'm wait - ing, give me.

# Growing on Me

**Words and Music by Justin David Hawkins, Daniel Francis Hawkins,
Edwin James Graham and Francis Gilles Poullain-Patterson**

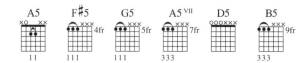

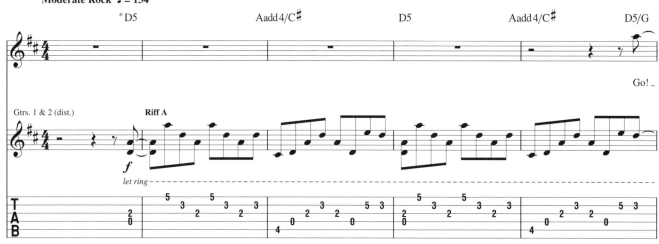

Drop D tuning:
(low to high) D-A-D-G-B-E

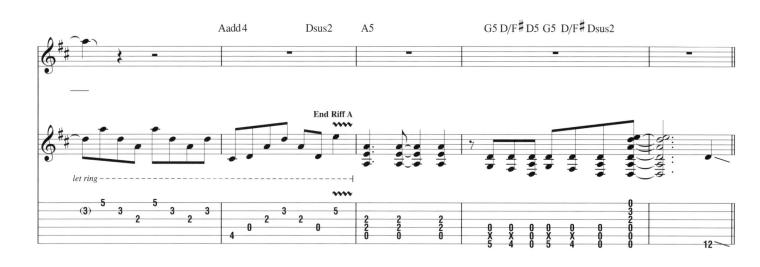

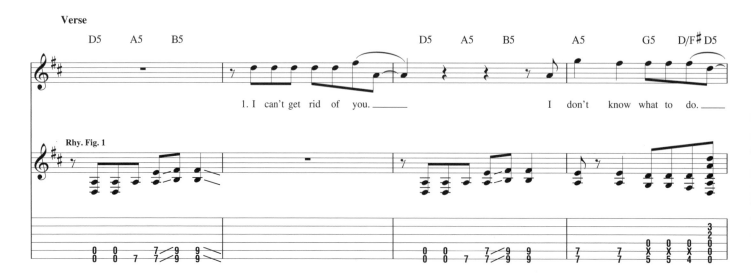

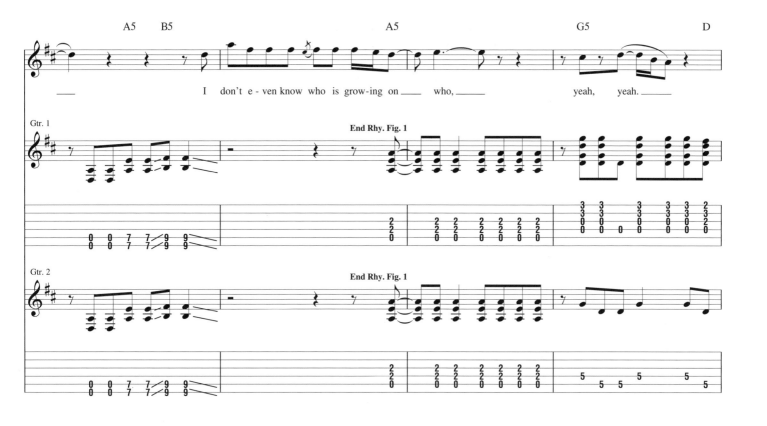

I don't e-ven know who is grow-ing on ___ who, ___ yeah, yeah. ___

Gtr. 1

End Rhy. Fig. 1

Gtr. 2

End Rhy. Fig. 1

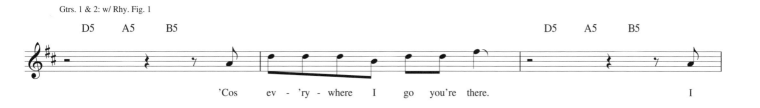

Gtrs. 1 & 2: w/ Rhy. Fig. 1

'Cos ev - 'ry - where I go you're there. I

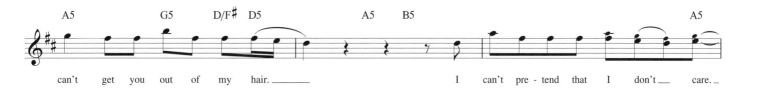

can't get you out of my hair. ___ I can't pre - tend that I don't ___ care. ___

It's not fair. ___

Rhy. Fig. 2

Gtrs. 1 & 2

End Rhy. Fig. 2

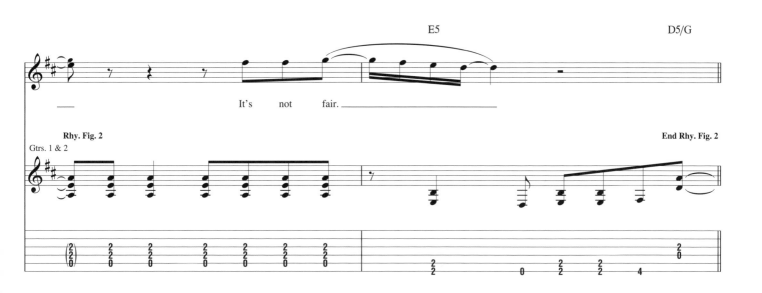

**Pre-Chorus**

Gtrs. 1 & 2: w/ Riff A

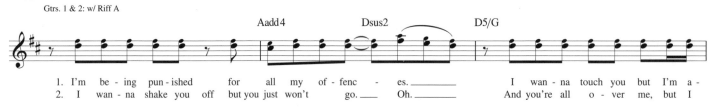

1. I'm be-ing pun-ished for all my of-fenc-es. _____ I wan-na touch you but I'm a-
2. I wan-na shake you off but you just won't go. ___ Oh. ___ And you're all o-ver me, but I

fraid of the con-se-quenc-es. I wan-na ban-ish you from whence you _____ came, but you're part
don't want an-y-one to know that you're at-tached to me, that's how you've_ grown. Won't you leave_

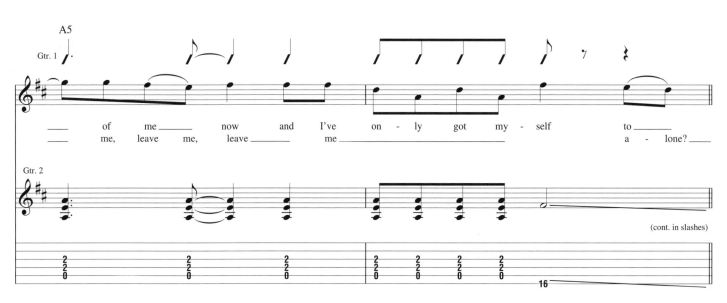

_____ of me _____ now and I've on-ly got my-self to _____
_____ me, leave me, leave _____ me _____ a-lone? _____

**Chorus**

Gtr. 3: w/ Rhy. Fig. 3 (2 times)

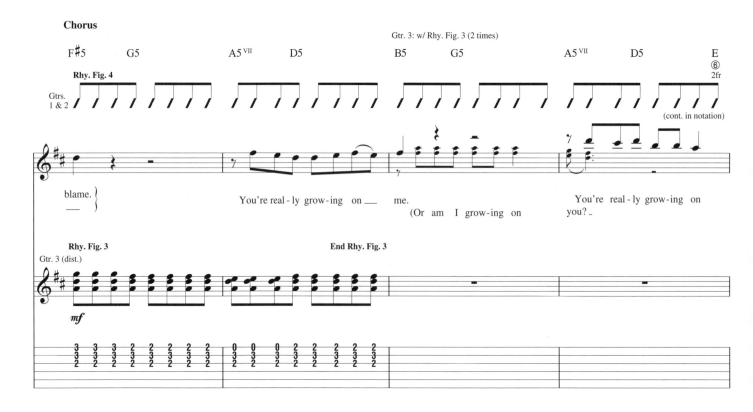

blame. _____ } You're real-ly grow-ing on _____ me. You're real-ly grow-ing on
(Or am I grow-ing on you? _

20

21

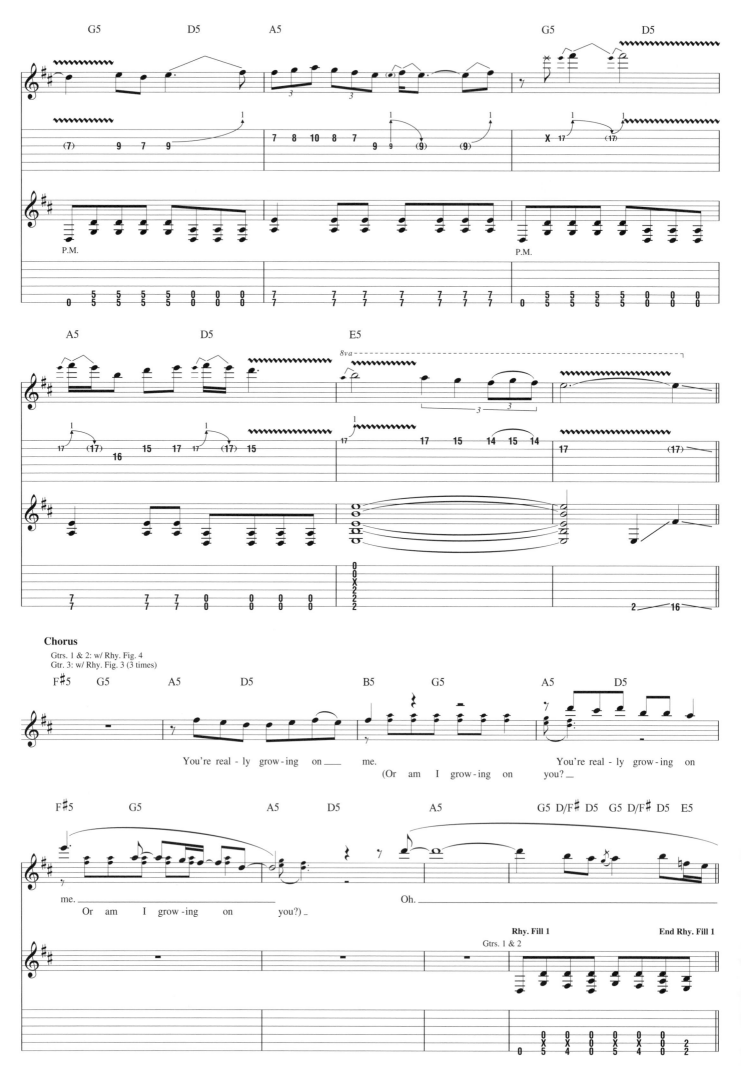

**Chorus**
Gtrs. 1 & 2: w/ Rhy. Fig. 4
Gtr. 3: w/ Rhy. Fig. 3 (3 times)

You're real-ly grow-ing on ___ me.
(Or am I grow-ing on you? ___

me. ___
Or am I grow-ing on you?) ___

Oh. ___

Rhy. Fill 1          End Rhy. Fill 1
Gtrs. 1 & 2

**Outro-Guitar Solo**

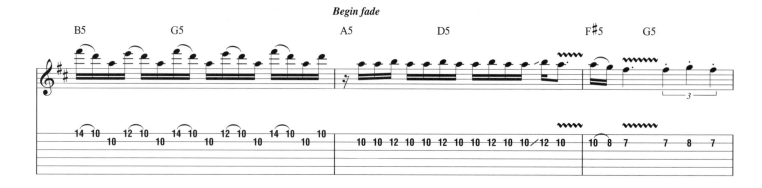

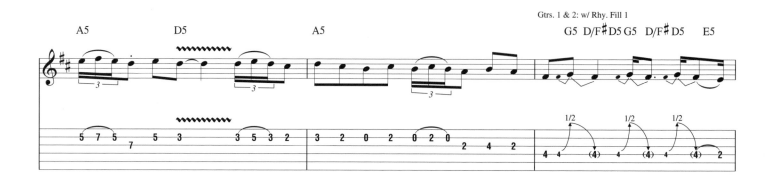

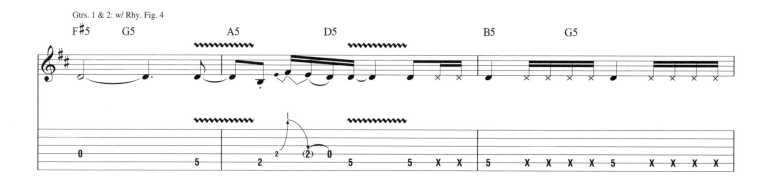

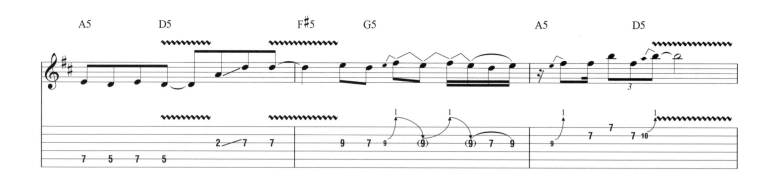

# (Can't Get My) Head Around You

**Words and Music by The Offspring**

E5

34

**Intro**
**Moderately fast Rock** ♩ = 144

**Verse**

1. Deep in-side your soul, there's a hole you don't want to see.

Gtrs. 1 & 2: w/ Rhy. Fig. 1 (2 times)

Ev-'ry sin-gle day, what you say makes no sense to me. E-ven though I try, I can't get my head a-round

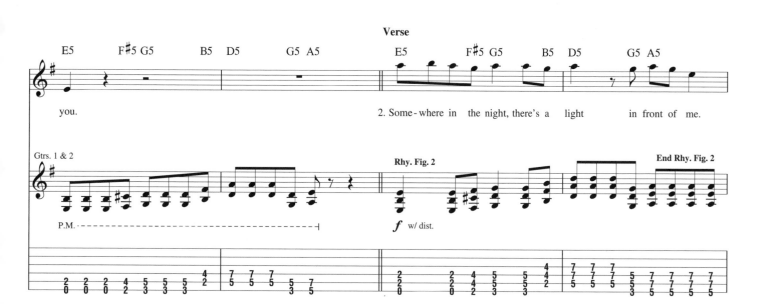

you.

2. Some-where in the night, there's a light in front of me.

Heav-en up a-bove, with a shove a-ban-dons me. And e-ven though I try, I

fall in the riv-er of you. You man-age to bring me down

**Chorus**

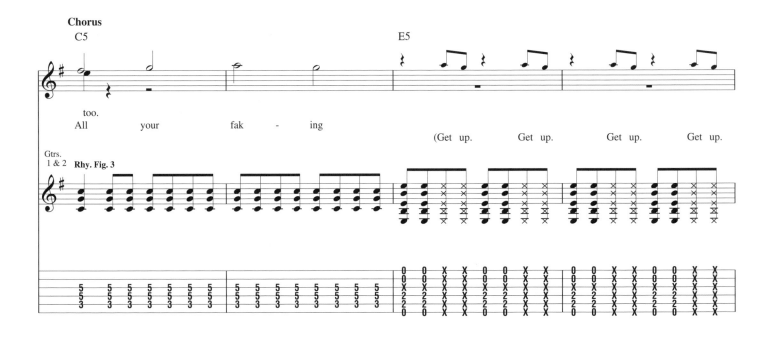

too. All your fak-ing

(Get up. Get up. Get up. Get up.

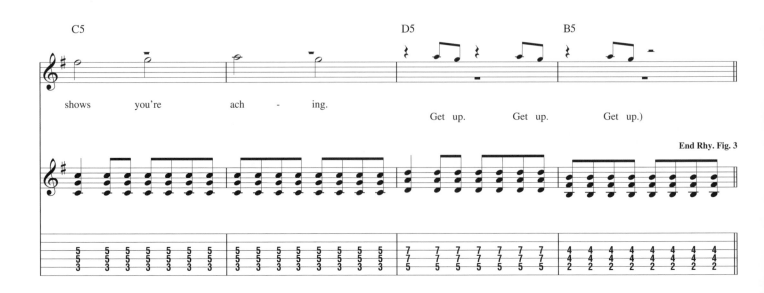

shows you're ach-ing.

Get up. Get up. Get up.)

**End Rhy. Fig. 3**

## Verse

Gtrs. 1 & 2: w/ Rhy. Fig. 2 (3 times)

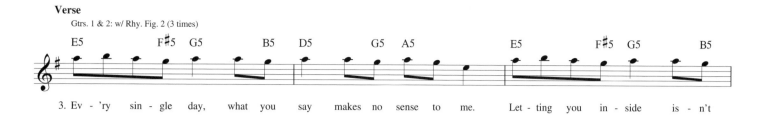

3. Ev - 'ry sin - gle day, what you say makes no sense to me. Let - ting you in - side is - n't

right ('cause) you'll mess with me. I nev - er real - ly know what's real - ly go - ing on in - side

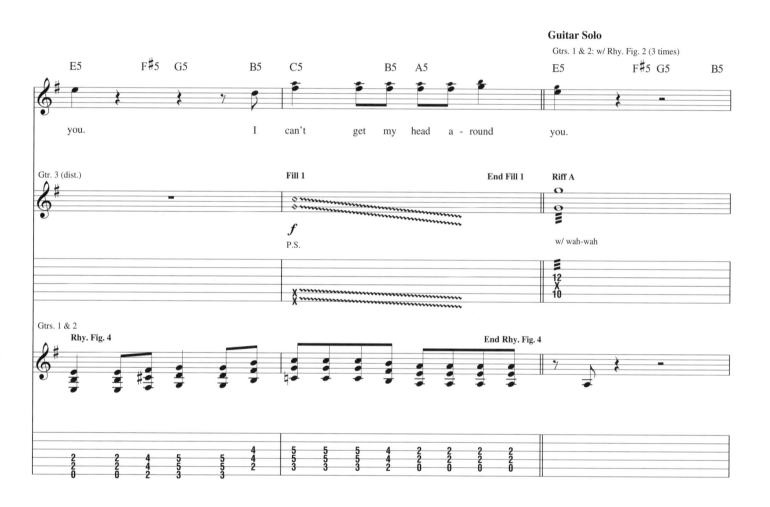

**Guitar Solo**

Gtrs. 1 & 2: w/ Rhy. Fig. 2 (3 times)

you. I can't get my head a - round you.

Gtr. 3 (dist.)

Fill 1    End Fill 1    Riff A

_f_

P.S.    w/ wah-wah

Gtrs. 1 & 2

Rhy. Fig. 4    End Rhy. Fig. 4

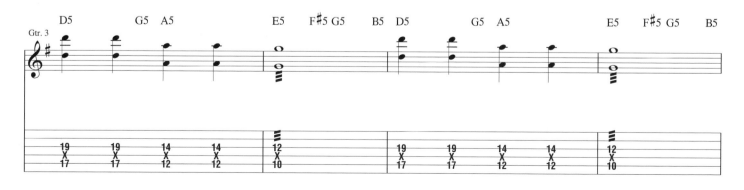

Gtr. 3

D5                G5   A5               E5

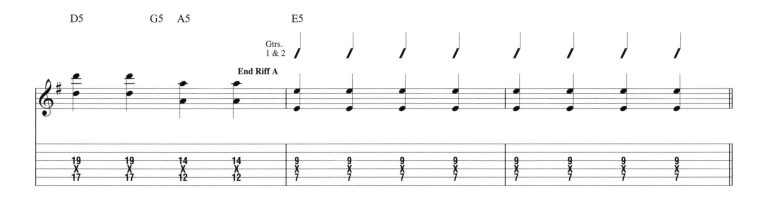

## Chorus

Gtrs. 1 & 2: w/ Rhy. Fig. 3
Gtr. 3 tacet

C5                                  E5

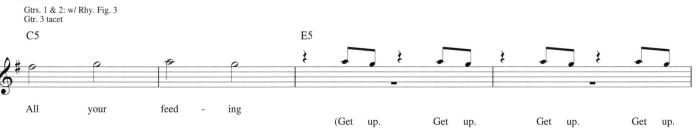

All       your       feed -    ing

(Get up.       Get up.       Get up.       Get up.

C5                                    D5                    B5

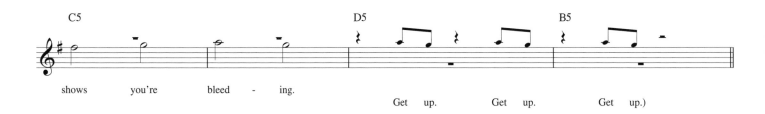

shows     you're     bleed -    ing.

Get up.       Get up.       Get up.)

## Verse

*Gtrs. 1 & 2: w/ Rhy. Fig. 1 (3 times)

E5           F#5  G5         B5    D5        G5  A5                E5          F#5  G5        B5

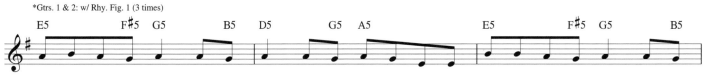

4. Deep in - side your soul, there's a    hole   you don't want to   see. You're  cov - er - ing     it      up     like    a

*Dist. off, *mp* .

D5         G5  A5                E5          F#5  G5        B5    D5        G5  A5

cut    with    the    likes   of    me.    You know I've  real - ly tried,      I   can't   do  an - y - more a - bout

E5               N.C.

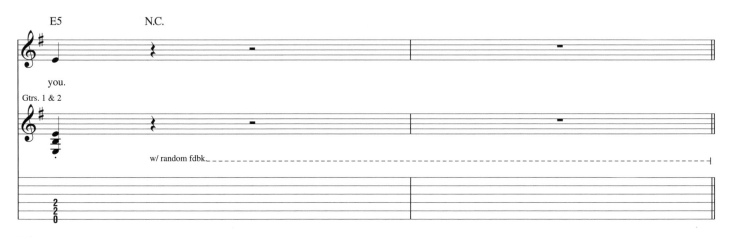

you.

Gtrs. 1 & 2

w/ random fdbk

## Outro

*Gtrs. 1 & 2: w/: Rhy. Fig. 2 (3 times)

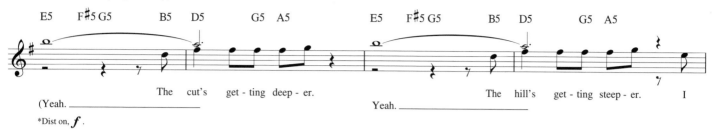

The cut's get-ting deep-er. The hill's get-ting steep-er. I

(Yeah. Yeah.

*Dist on, $f$.

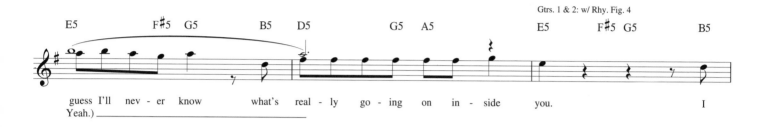

guess I'll nev-er know what's real-ly go-ing on in-side you. I
Yeah.)

Gtrs. 1 & 2: w/ Rhy. Fig. 4

Gtr. 3: w/ Fill 1

Gtrs. 1 & 2: w/ Rhy. Fig. 2 (3 times)
Gtr. 3: w/ Riff A

can't get my head a-round you. I can't get my head a-round

you. I can't get my head a-round you. I can't get my head a-round

you.

Gtr. 3

# Here Without You

**Words and Music by Brad Arnold, Matthew Darrick Roberts, Christopher Lee Henderson and Robert Todd Harrell**

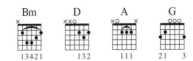

Tune down 1/2 step:
(low to high) Eb-Ab-Db-Gb-Bb-Eb

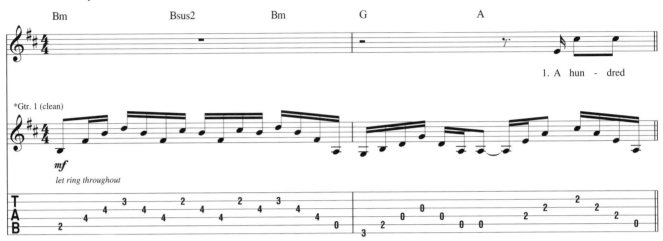

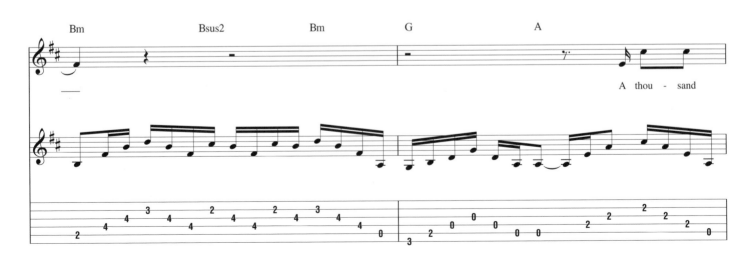

# I Miss You

**Words and Music by Travis Barker, Tom De Longe and Mark Hoppus**

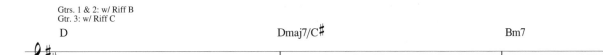

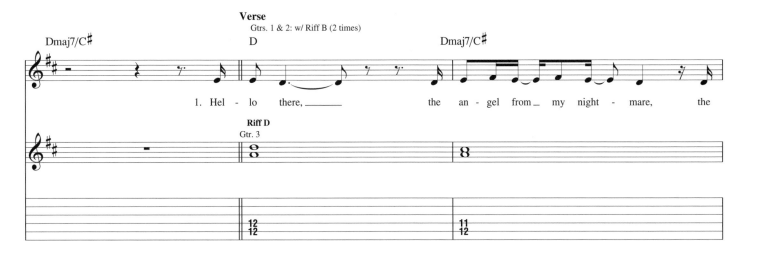

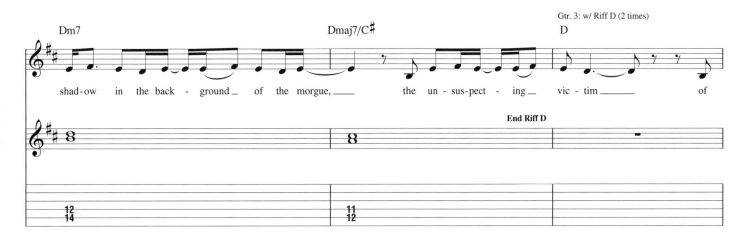

in the night \_\_\_ we'll wish this nev - er ends, \_\_\_ we'll wish this nev - er ends, \_\_\_

End Riff E

Chorus

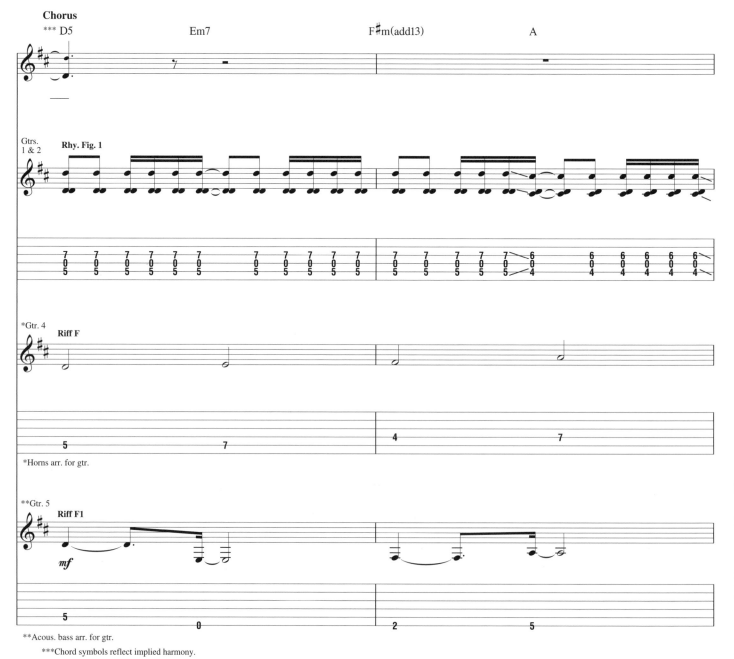

\*Horns arr. for gtr.

\*\*Acous. bass arr. for gtr.

\*\*\*Chord symbols reflect implied harmony.

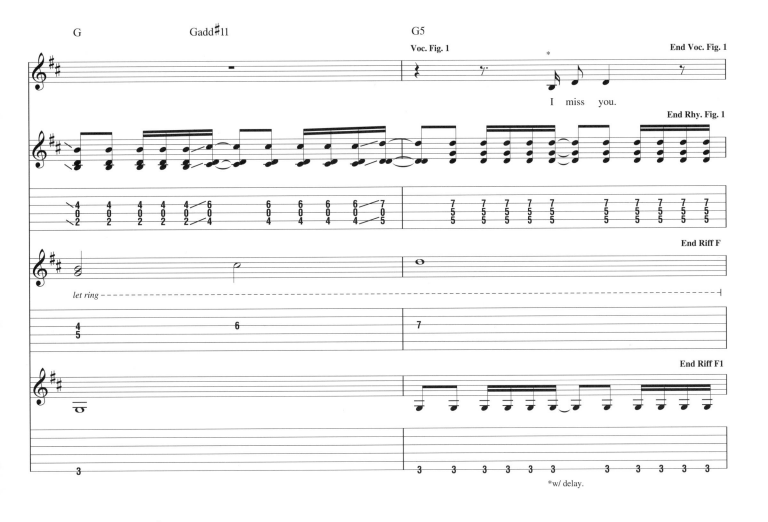

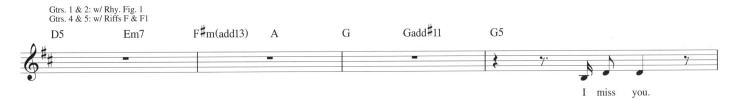

I'm so ___ sor - ry, I can-not sleep, I can-not dream to - night. ___ I need some-bod - y. And,

**End Riff G**

Gtrs. 1 & 2: w/ Riff B (2 times)
Gtr. 6: w/ Riff G (3 times)

al - ways ___ this sick, strange ___ dark - ness comes creep-ing on, ___ so haunt - ing ev - 'ry

time. And as I stared ___ I count - ed ___ the webs from all ___ the spi - ders

catch - ing things and eat - ing their ___ in - sides, like in - de - ci - sion to call ___ you and

Gtrs. 1 & 2: w/ Riff E

hear your voice ___ of trea - son. Will you come home ___ and stop this pain to - night? ___ Stop this pain to - night. ___

**Chorus**

Gtrs. 1 & 2: w/ Rhy. Fig. 1 (2 times)
Gtrs. 4 & 5: w/ Riffs F & F1

Gtr. 6 tacet

Voc.: w/ Voc. Fig. 1

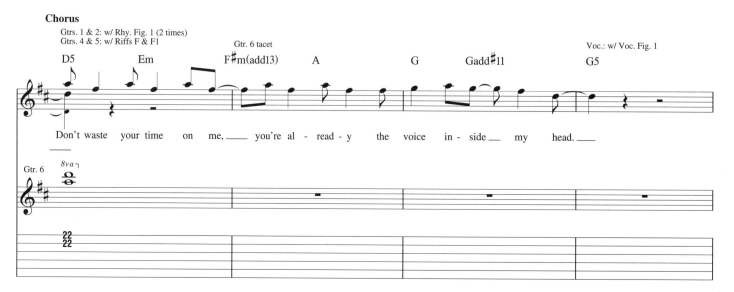

Don't waste your time on me, ___ you're al - read - y the voice in - side ___ my head. ___

Gtr. 6

40

So waste your time on me, ___ you're al - read - y the voice in - side ___ my head. ___

**Interlude**

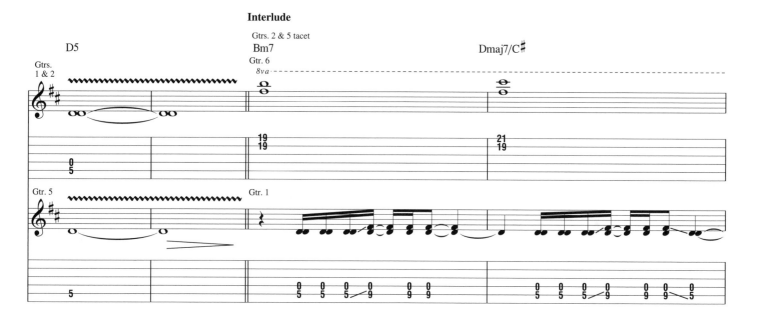

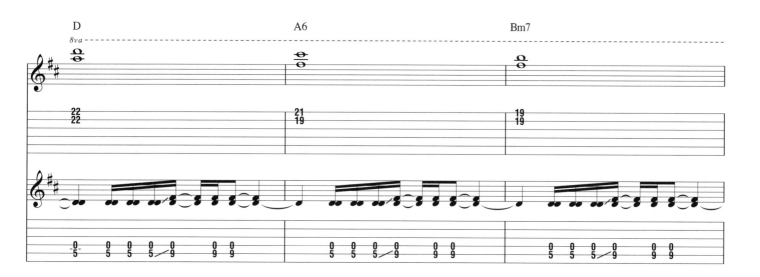

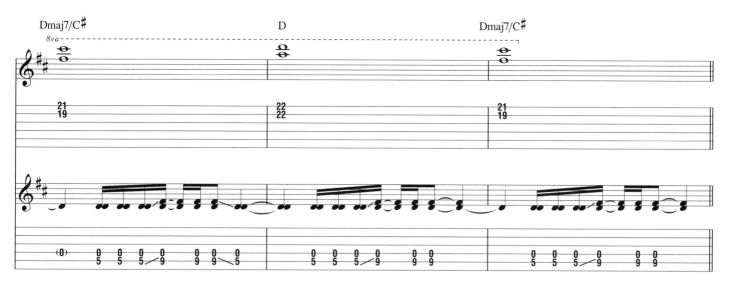

**Chorus**
Gtrs. 1 & 2: w/ Rhy. Fig. 1 (2 times)
Gtr. 4: w/ Riff F (2 times)
Gtr. 6 tacet

Voc.: w/ Voc. Fig. 1

Don't waste your time on me ____ you're al - read - y the voice in - side ____ my head. ____

Voc.: w/ Voc. Fig. 1

So waste your time on me, ____ you're al - read - y the voice in - side ____ my head. ____

**Outro-Piano Solo**
Gtrs. 1 & 2: w/ Rhy. Fig. 1 (till fade)
Gtr. 4: w/ Riff F (till fade)

Voc.: w/ Voc. Fig. 1

Voc.: w/ Voc. Fig. 1

*Begin fade*

Voc.: w/ Voc. Fig. 1

*Fade out*

Voc.: w/ Voc. Fig. 1

# Just Like You

## Words and Music by Three Days Grace and Gavin Brown

Drop D tuning, down 1/2 step:
(low to high) Db-Ab-Db-Gb-Bb-Eb

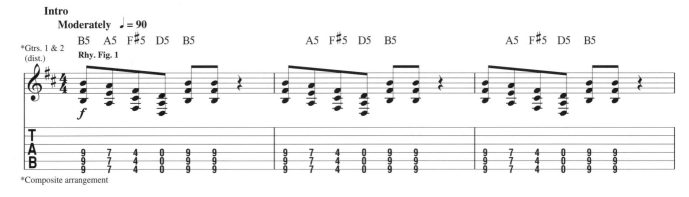

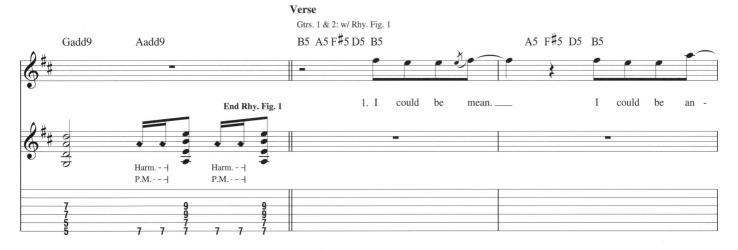

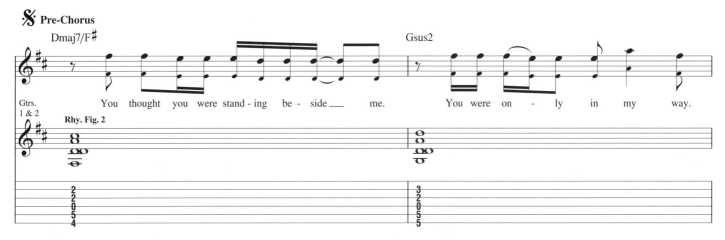

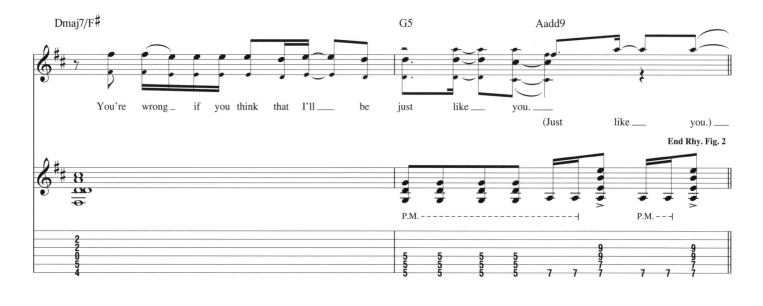

You're wrong _ if you think that I'll _ be just like _ you.

(Just like _ you.)

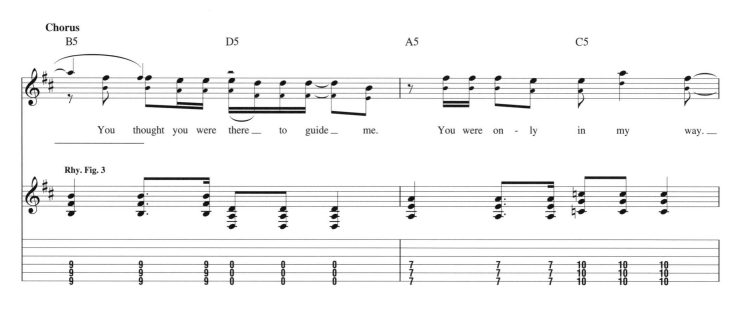

**Chorus**

You thought you were there _ to guide _ me. You were on - ly in my way. _

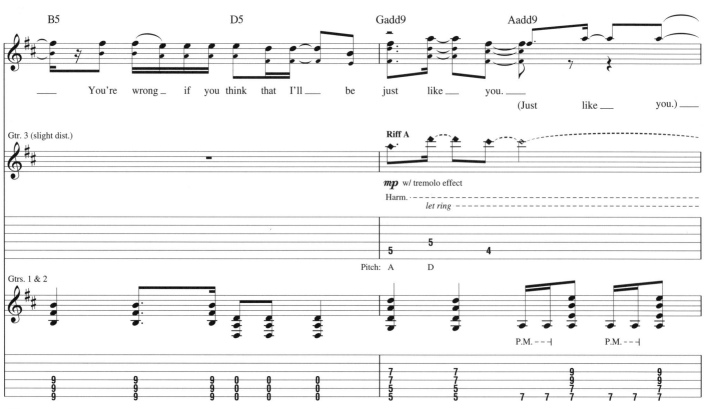

_ You're wrong _ if you think that I'll _ be just like _ you. _

(Just like _ you.)

**Chorus**

*Gtrs. 1 & 2: w/ Rhy. Fig. 3

*Gtr. 2, tremolo off.

Gtr. 3: w/ Riff A

**Verse**

Gtrs. 1 & 2: w/ Rhy. Fig. 1

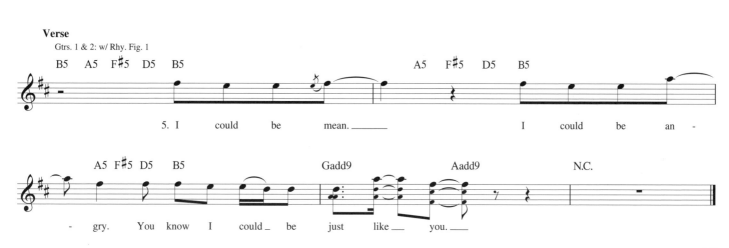

# Last Train Home

**Words and Music by Michael Lewis, Ian Watkins, Richard Oliver, Lee Gaze, Stuart Richardson and Michael Chiplin**

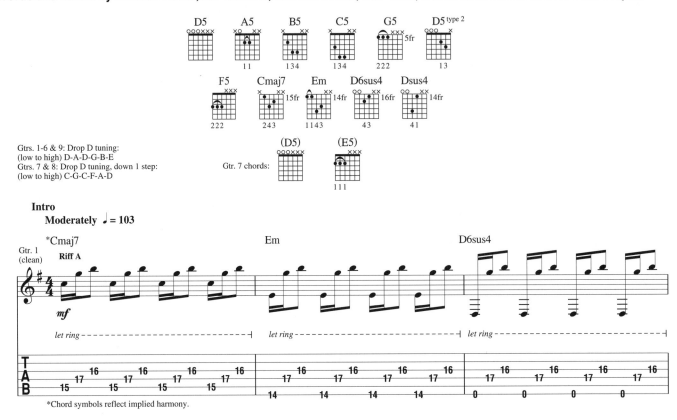

Gtrs. 1-6 & 9: Drop D tuning:
(low to high) D-A-D-G-B-E
Gtrs. 7 & 8: Drop D tuning, down 1 step:
(low to high) C-G-C-F-A-D

Gtr. 7 chords:

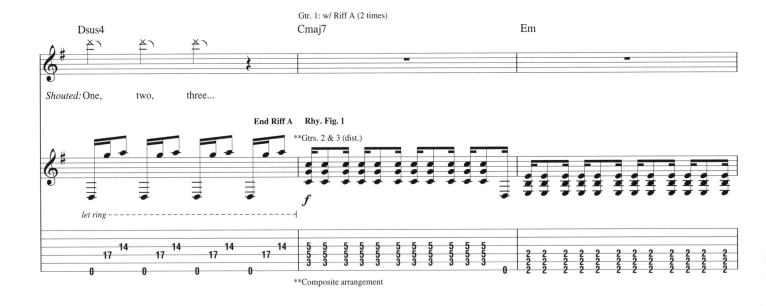

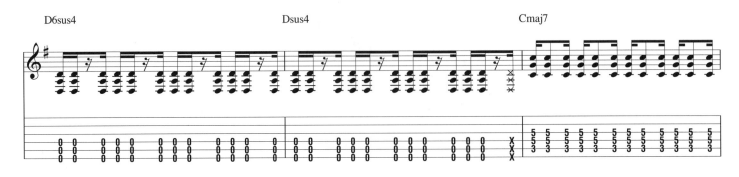

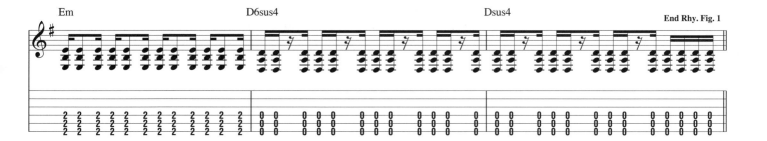

**Verse**

Gtrs. 2 & 3 tacet

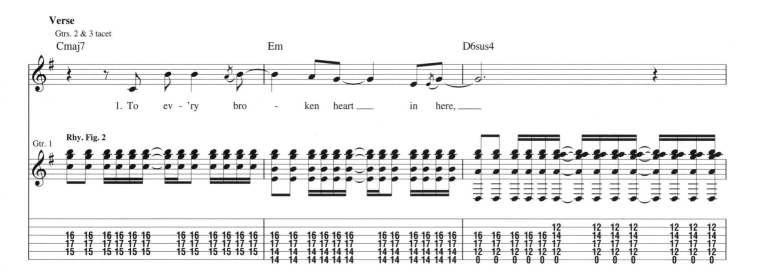

1. To ev - 'ry bro - ken heart ___ in here, ___

love ___ was ___ once ___ a part, ___ but now ___

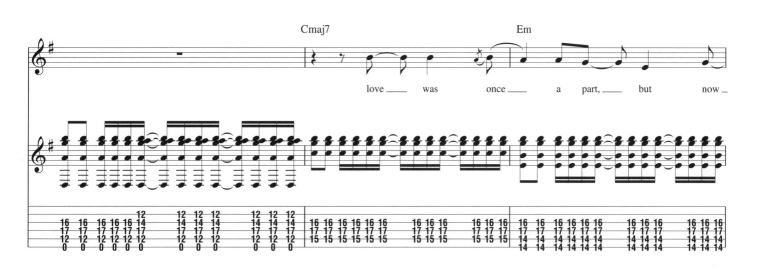

___ it's ___ dis - ap - peared. ___ She told me that it's

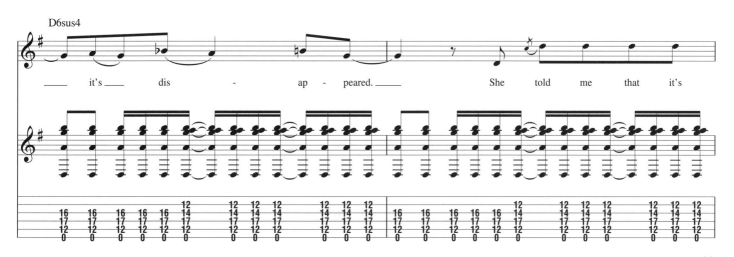

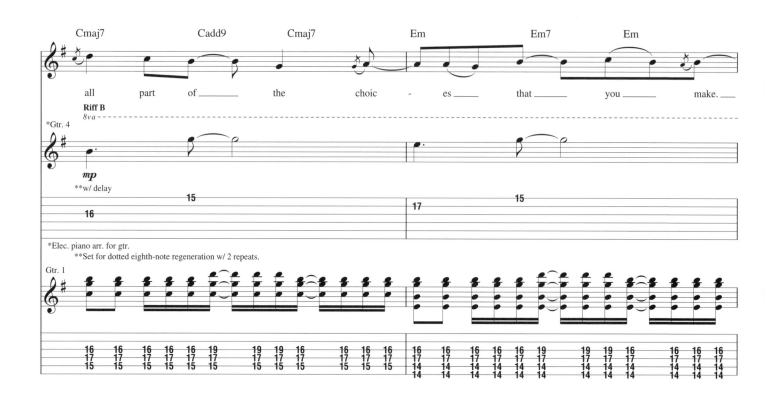

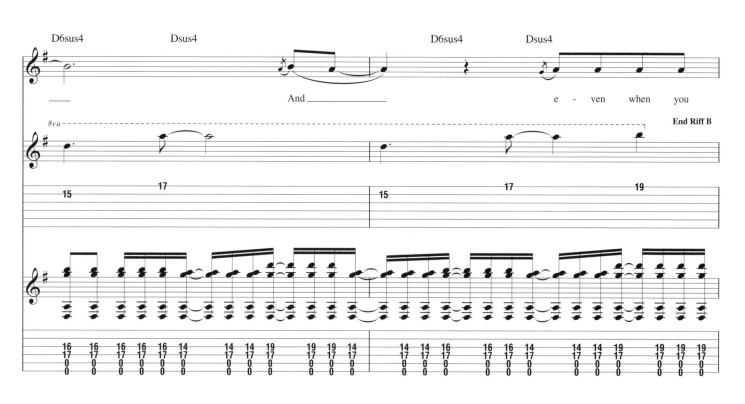

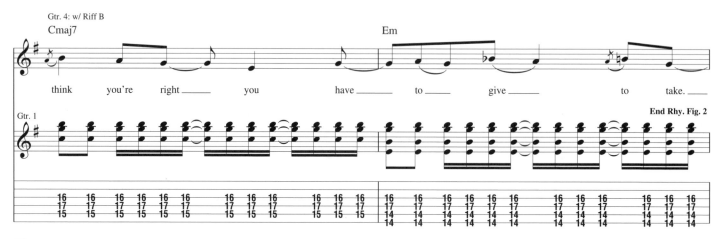

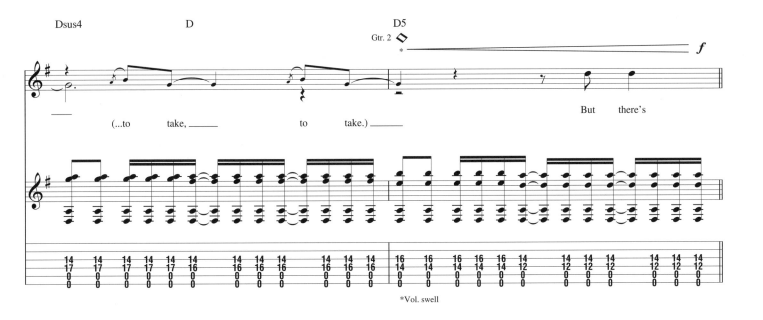

*Vol. swell

**𝄋 Pre-Chorus**
**Double-time feel**
Gtrs. 1 & 4 tacet

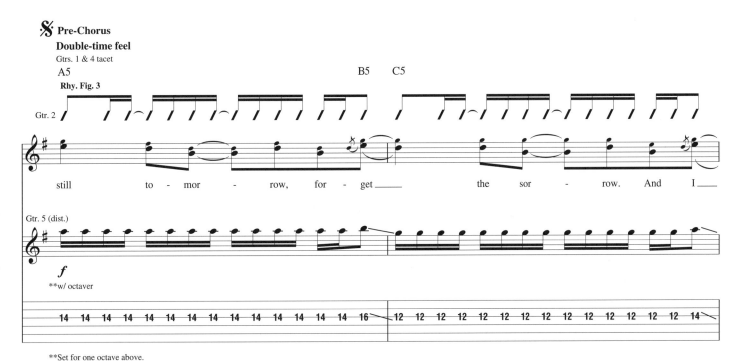

**Set for one octave above.

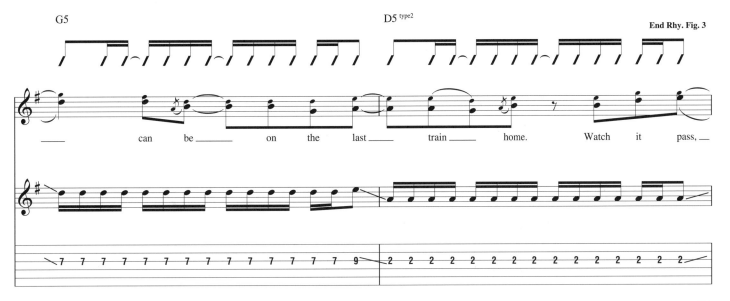

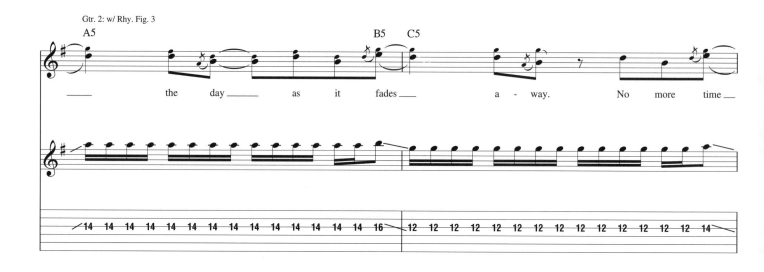

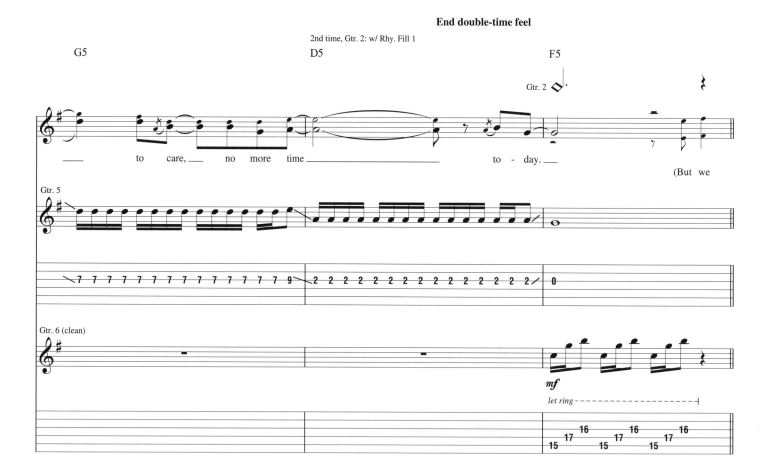

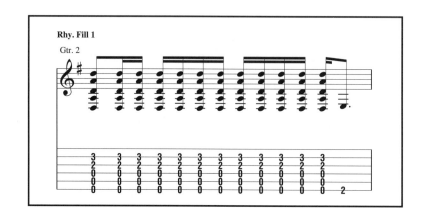

**Chorus**

1st time, Gtr. 1: w/ Riff A (2 times)
1st time, Gtrs. 2 & 3: w/ Rhy. Fig. 1
2nd time, Gtr. 1: w/ Riff A (1 3/4 times)
2nd time, Gtrs. 2 & 3: w/ Rhy. Fig. 1 (1st 7 meas.)
Gtrs. 5 & 6 tacet

If we're go-ing no - where, _ if it's not e - nough. _____

Voc. Fig. 1

sing, _____ yeah, we sing, _____ and we

*To Coda* ⊕

Sing with - out a rea - son to ev - er fall _____ in _____ love. ____

**End Voc. Fig. 1**

sing.) _____

**Verse**

Gtr. 1: w/ Rhy Fig. 2

2. I won - der _ if _____ you're lis - ten - ing, _____ pick - ing up on _____

Gtr. 4

*8va*

Gtr. 4: w/ Riff B (2 3/4 times)

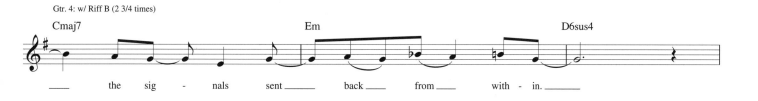

_____ the sig - nals sent _____ back _____ from _____ with - in. _____

Some-times it feels like I don't real - ly know ___ what's go - ing ___ on. ___

Time and time a - gain it seems _ like ev - 'ry - thing _ is _

D.S. al Coda

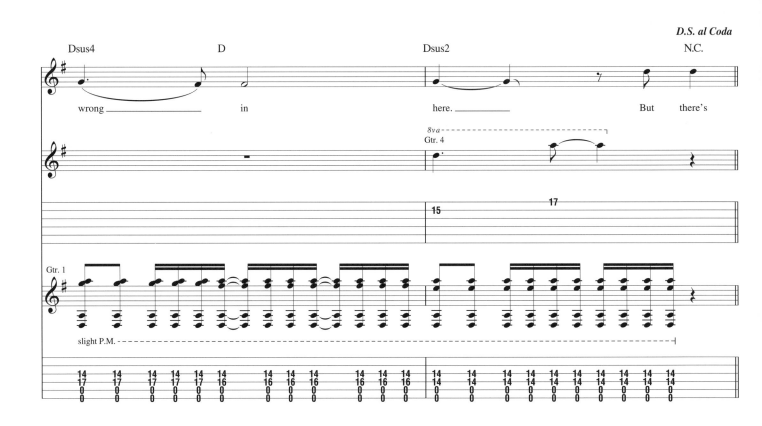

wrong _ in here. _ But there's

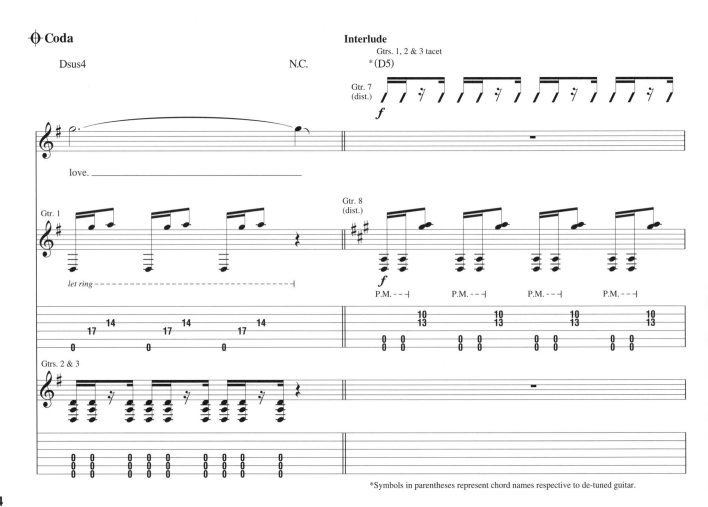

love. _

Interlude

Gtrs. 1, 2 & 3 tacet

*Symbols in parentheses represent chord names respective to de-tuned guitar.

54

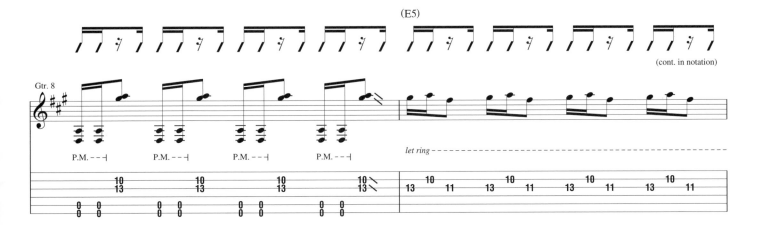

(E5)

(cont. in notation)

**Chorus**

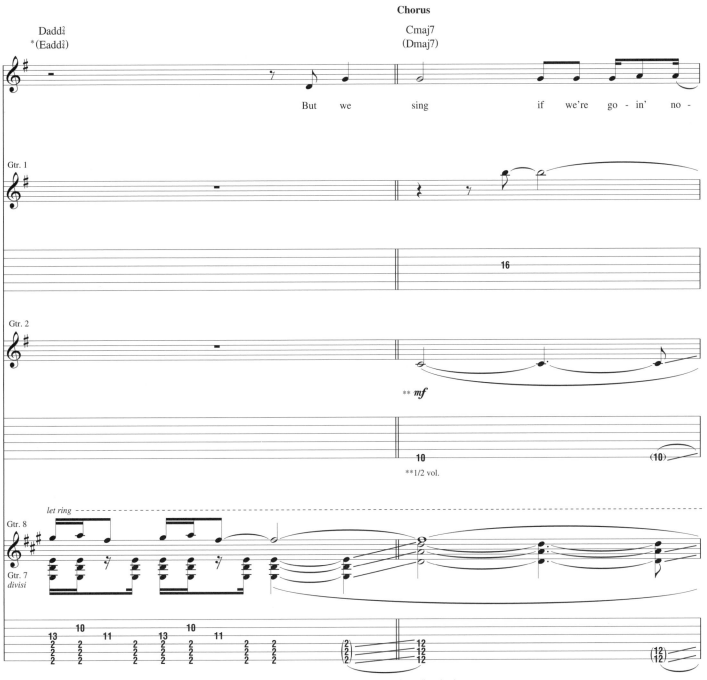

But we sing if we're go-in' no-

*Symbols in parentheses represent chord names respective to de-tuned guitar. Symbols above represent actual sounding chords.

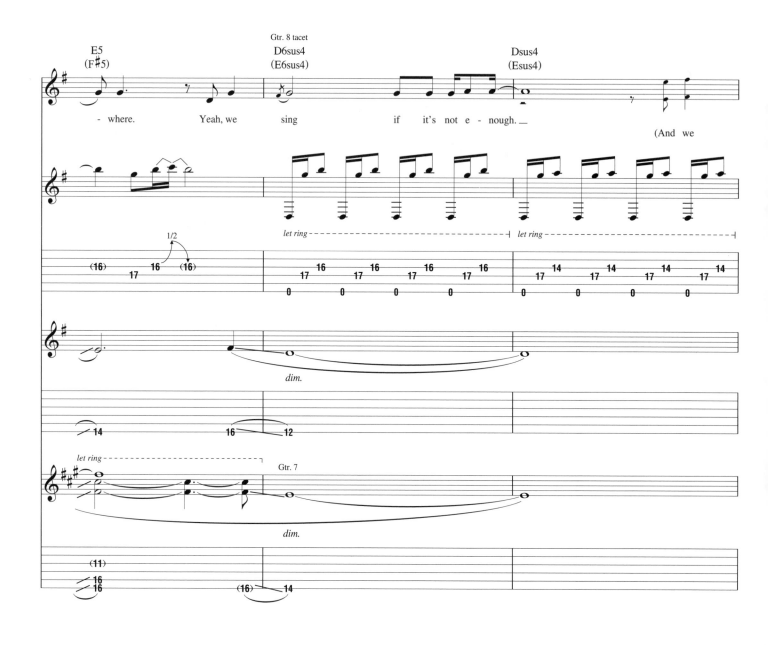

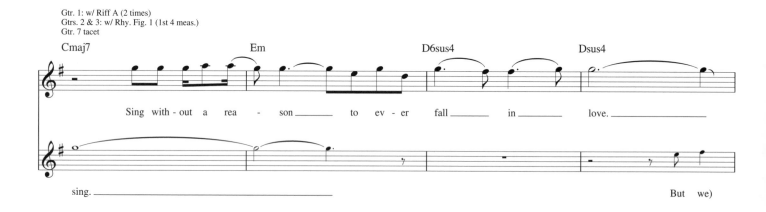

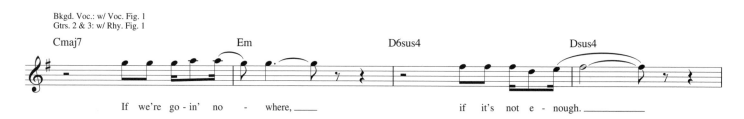

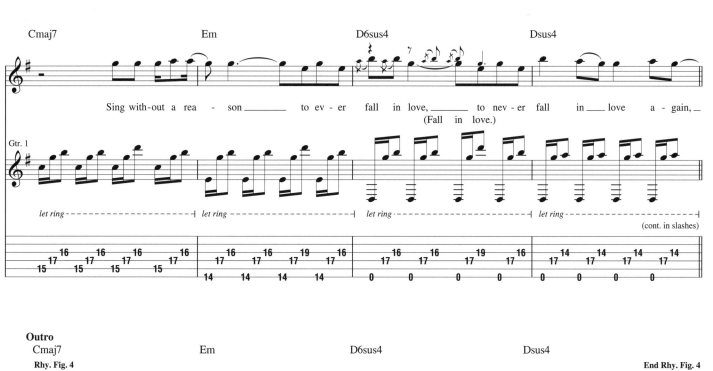

Sing with-out a rea - son ____ to ev - er fall in love, ____ to nev - er fall in ____ love a - gain, ____
(Fall in love.)

**Outro**

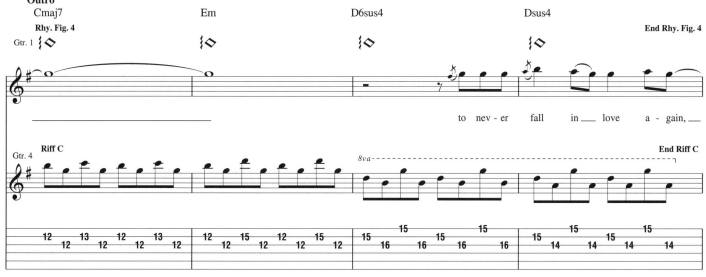

to nev - er fall in ____ love a - gain, ____

Gtr. 1:w/ Rhy. Fig. 4
Gtr. 4: w/ Riff C

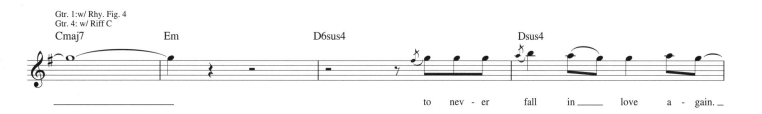

to nev - er fall in ____ love a - gain. ____

*Segue to "Make a Move"*

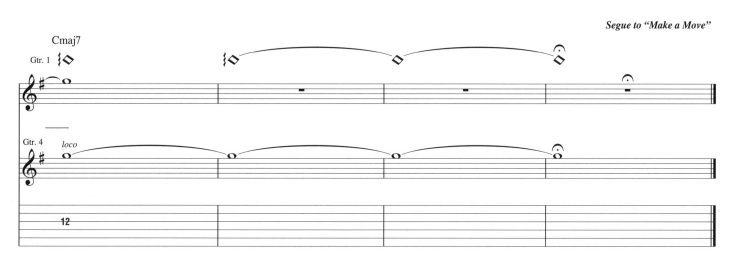

# Maps

**Words and Music by Karen Orzolek, Nick Zinner and Brian Chase**

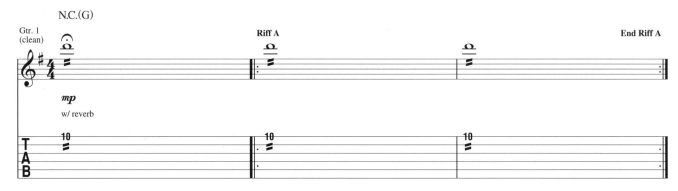

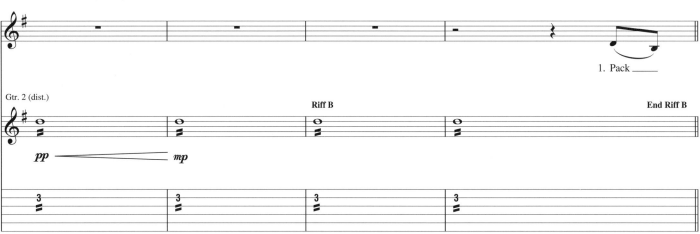

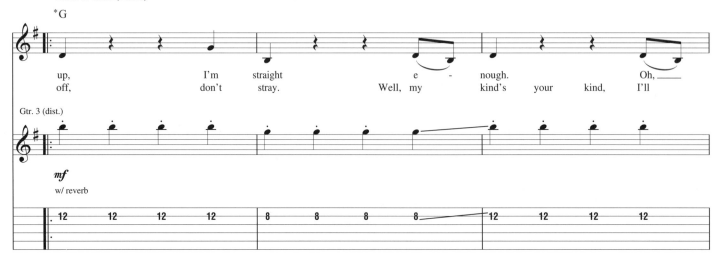

*Chord symbols reflect implied harmony.

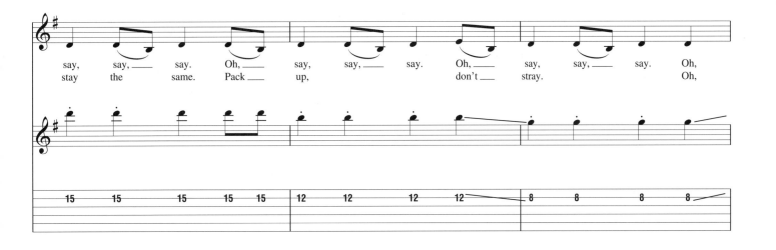

say, say, say. Oh, say, say, say. Oh, say, say, say. Oh,
stay the same. Pack up, don't stray. Oh,

15  15  15  15  15  12  12  12  12  8  8  8  8

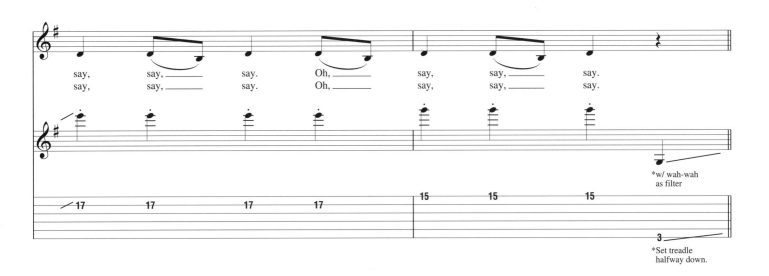

say, say, say. Oh, say, say, say.
say, say, say. Oh, say, say, say.

*w/ wah-wah
as filter

17  17  17  17  15  15  15

3

*Set treadle
halfway down.

§ **Chorus**

1st time, Gtr. 1: w/ Riff A (4 times)
1st time, Gtr. 2: w/ Riff B (4 times)
2nd & 3rd times, Gtr. 1: w/ Riff A (8 times)
2nd & 3rd times, Gtr. 2: w/ Riff B (8 times)
3rd time, Gtr. 6 tacet

C5                                    G5

Wait,              they don't love you like I love you.

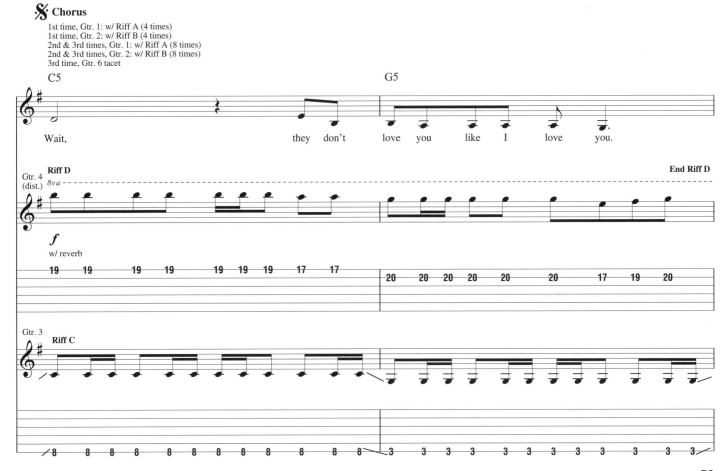

Gtr. 4    **Riff D**                                        **End Riff D**
(dist.) *8va- - - - - - - - - - - - - - - - - - - - - - - - - - -*

*f*
w/ reverb

19  19  19  19  19  19  19  17  17      20  20  20  20  20  20  17  19  20

Gtr. 3    **Riff C**

8  8  8  8  8  8  8  8  8  8  8      3  3  3  3  3  3  3  3  3  3

2nd time, Gtr. 4: w/ Riff D

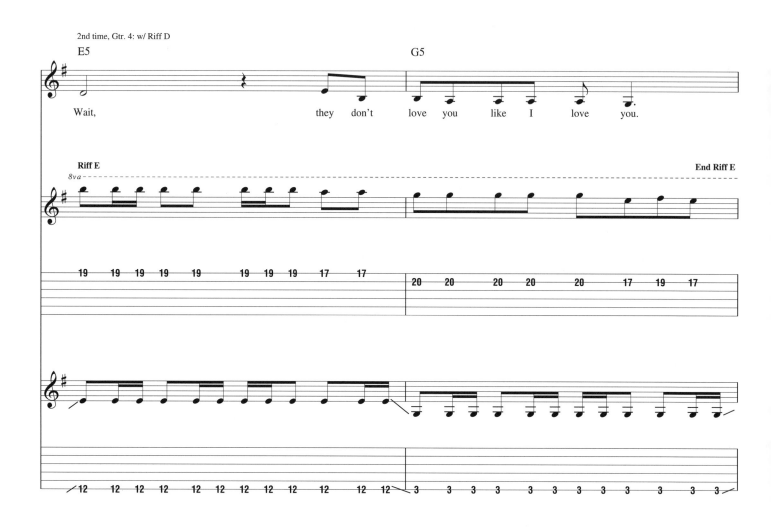

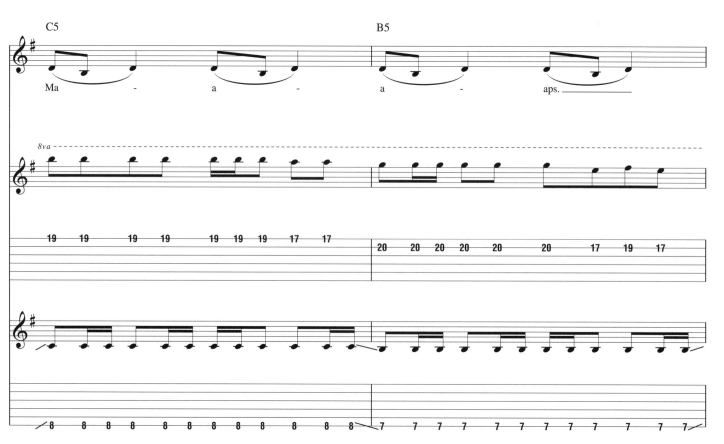

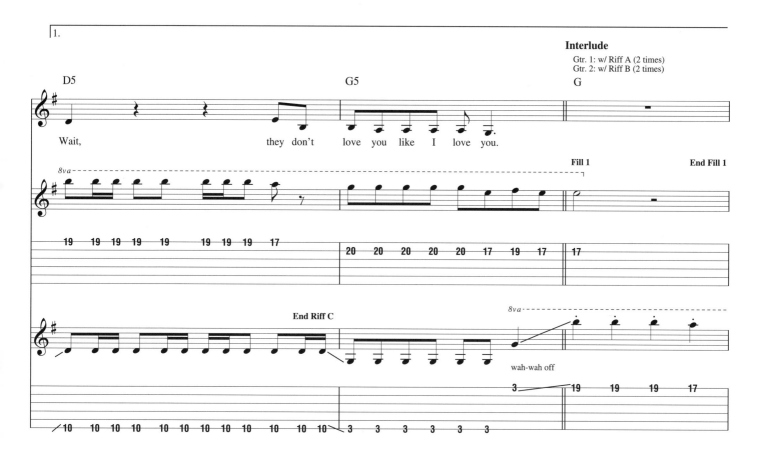

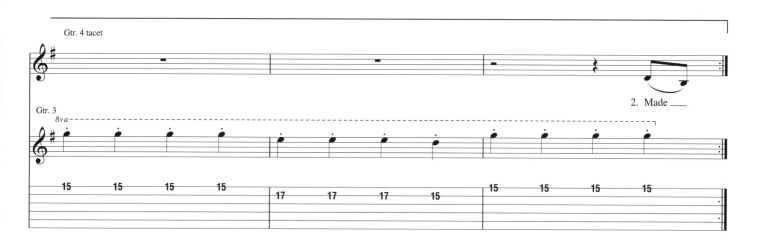

love you like I love you. Ma - a - a - aps. _____

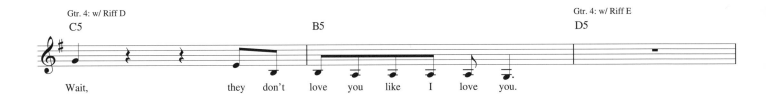

Wait, they don't love you like I love you.

**Interlude**

Gtr. 1: w/ Riff A (4 times)
Gtr. 2: w/ Riff B (4 times)
Gtr. 4: w/ Fill 1

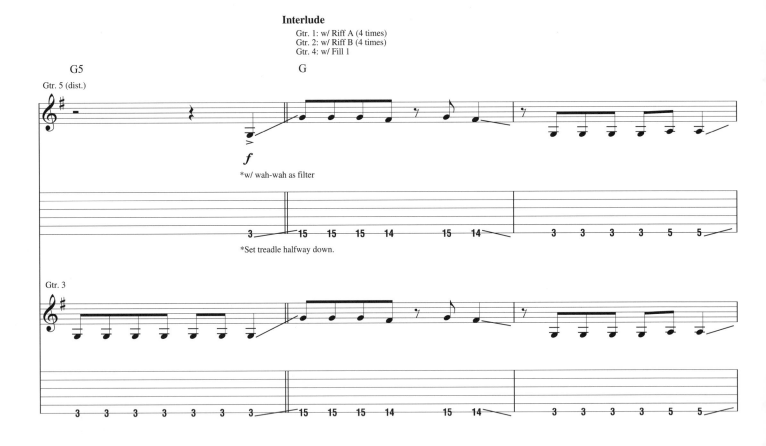

*w/ wah-wah as filter

*Set treadle halfway down.

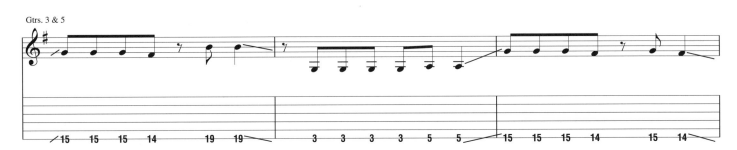

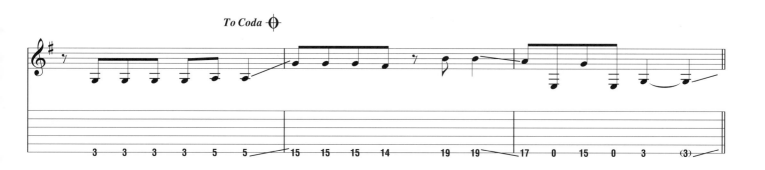

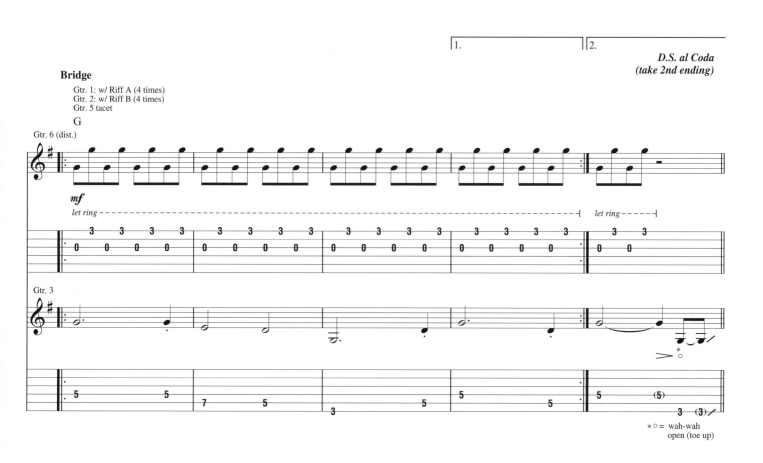

*○ = wah-wah
   open (toe up)

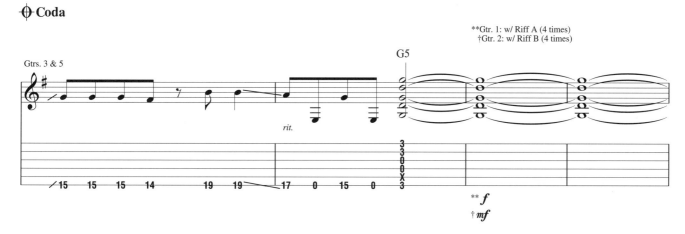

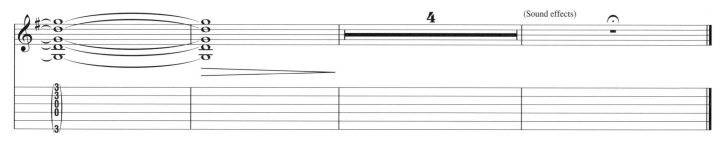

# Megalomaniac

**Words and Music by Brandon Boyd, Michael Einziger, Jose Pasillas II, Chris Kilmore and Ben Kenney**

Eb5

Intro

Moderately fast ♩ = 140

*G5

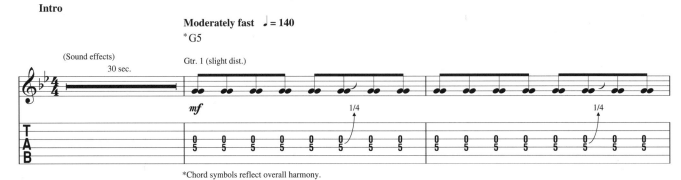

*Chord symbols reflect overall harmony.

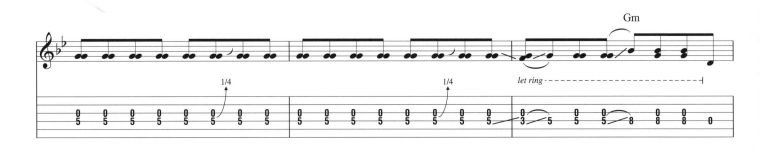

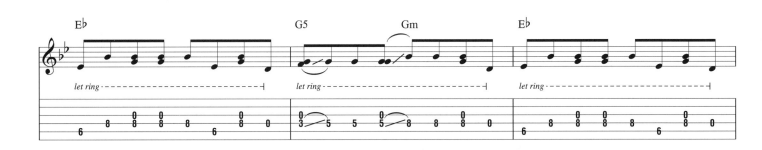

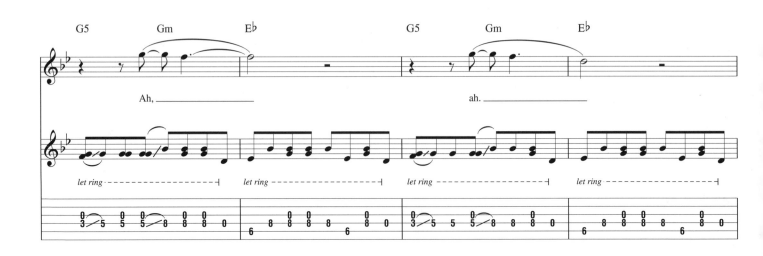

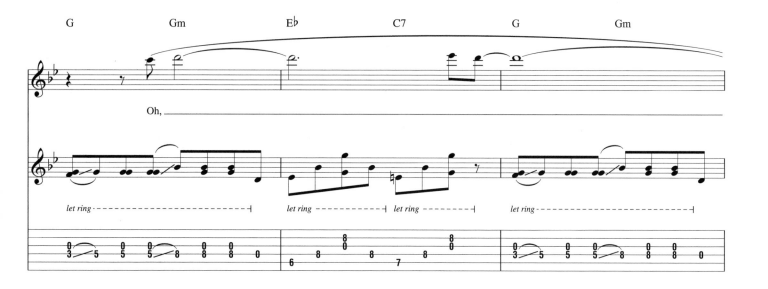

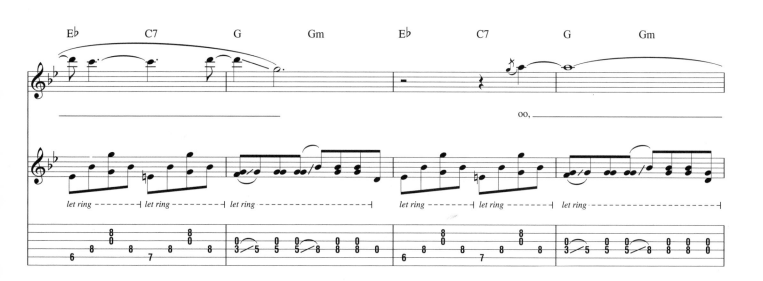

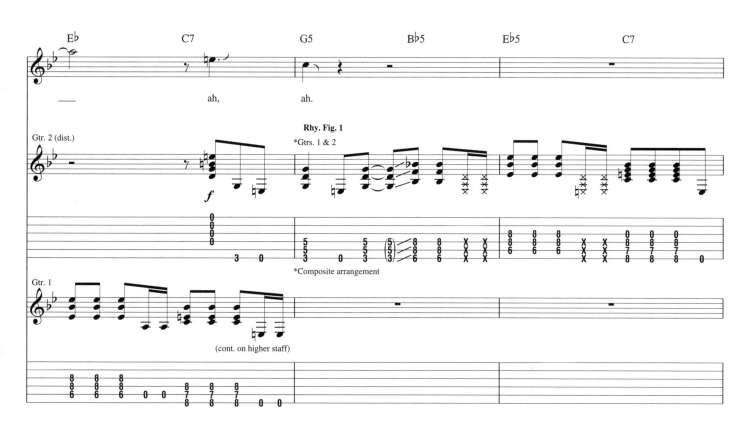

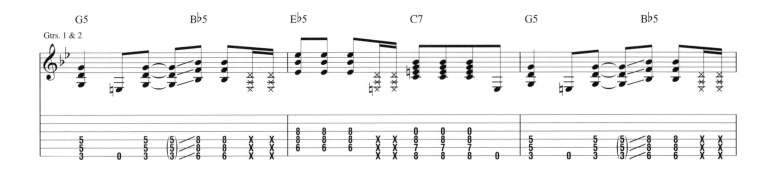

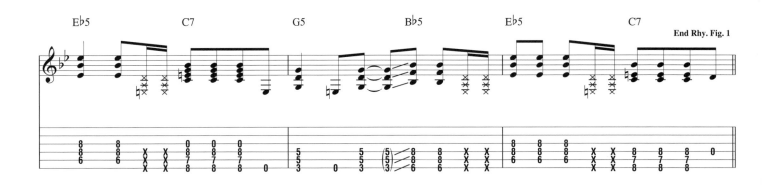

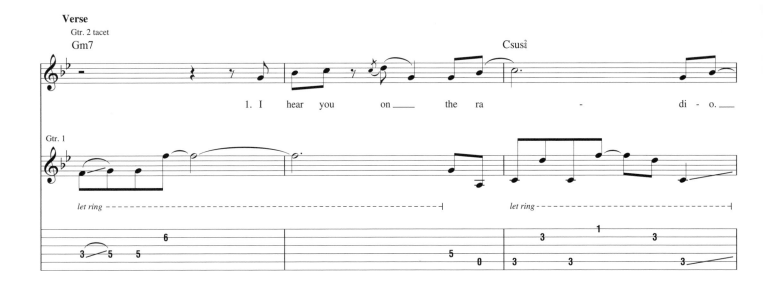

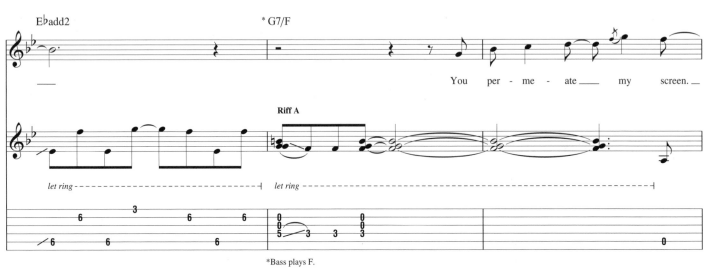

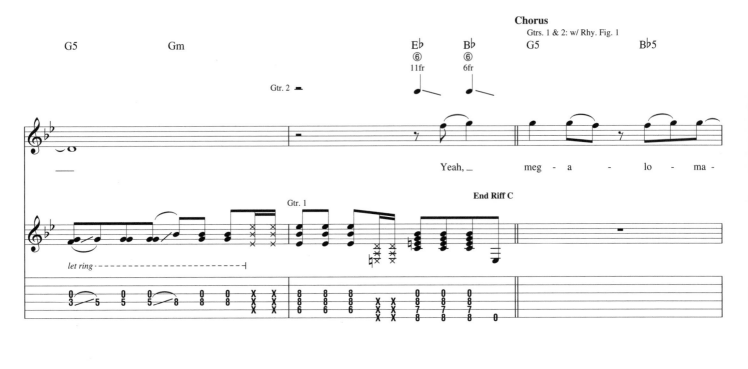

**Chorus**

Yeah, \_\_ meg - a - lo - ma -

- ni - ac, \_\_ you're no Je - sus, yeah, you're\_\_ no fuck - ing El - vis.

Wash your \_\_ hands clean of \_\_ your - self, ba - by, and step down, \_\_ step down, \_\_ step down. \_\_

**Interlude**

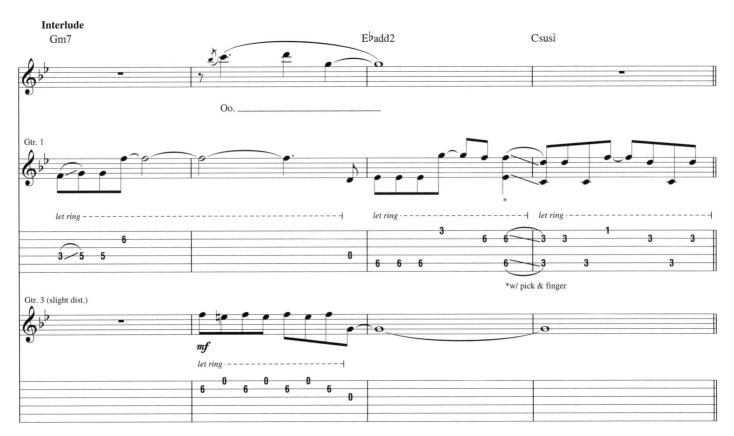

Oo. \_\_

*w/ pick & finger

**Verse**

2. If I were your ap - pend - ag - es

I'd hold o - pen your eyes so you would see

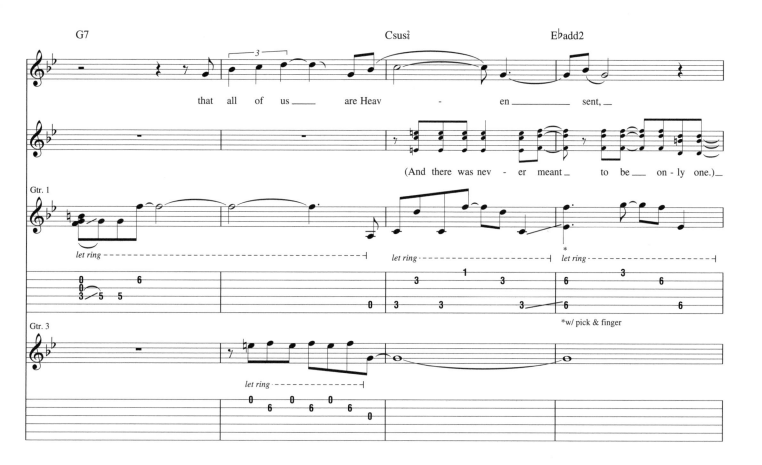

that all of us are Heav - en sent,

(And there was nev - er meant to be on - ly one.)

*w/ pick & finger

and there was nev - er meant to be on - ly one,
(Be on - ly one.)

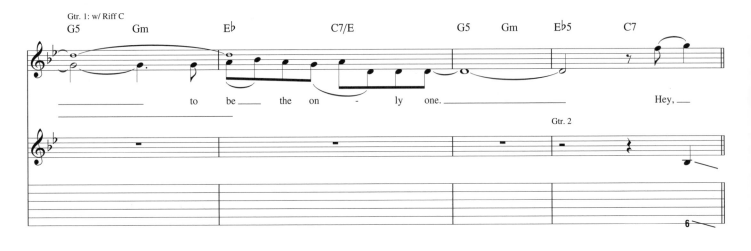

Gtr. 1: w/ Riff C

G5  Gm  E♭  C7/E  G5  Gm  E♭5  C7

to be the on - ly one.  Hey, —

Gtr. 2

6

## 𝄋 Chorus

Gtrs. 1 & 2: w/ Rhy. Fig. 1 (2 times)
2nd time, Gtrs. 1 & 2: w/ Rhy. Fig. 1 (1 7/8 times)

G5  B♭5  E♭5  C7  G5  B♭5  E♭5  C7

meg - a - lo - ma - ni - ac, — you're no Je - sus, yeah, you're — no fuck - ing El - vis.

G5  B♭5  E♭5  C7  G5  B♭5  E♭5  C7

Wash your — hands clean of — your-self, ba - by, and step down, — step down, — step down. —

Gtr. 4 (dist.)

𝆑

w/ step flanger

15  0

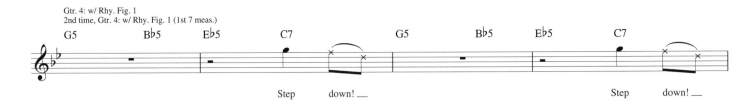

Gtr. 4: w/ Rhy. Fig. 1
2nd time, Gtr. 4: w/ Rhy. Fig. 1 (1st 7 meas.)

G5  B♭5  E♭5  C7  G5  B♭5  E♭5  C7

Step  down! —  Step  down! —

*To Coda* 🔶

**Interlude**

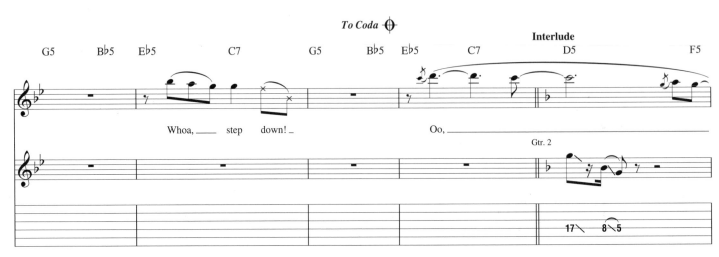

G5  B♭5  E♭5  C7  G5  B♭5  E♭5  C7  D5  F5

Whoa, — step down! —  Oo, —

Gtr. 2

17  8  5

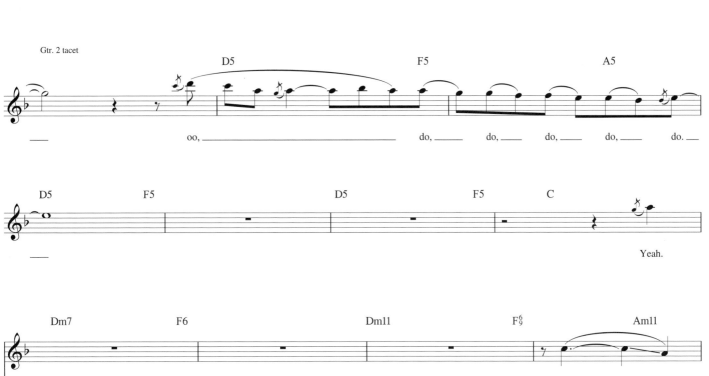

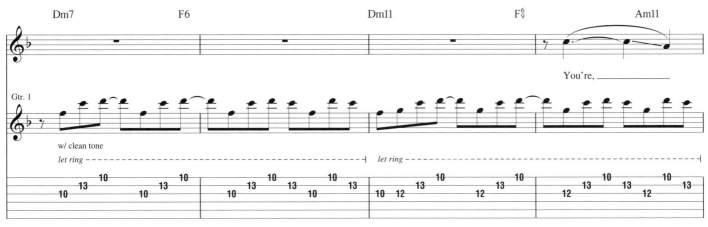

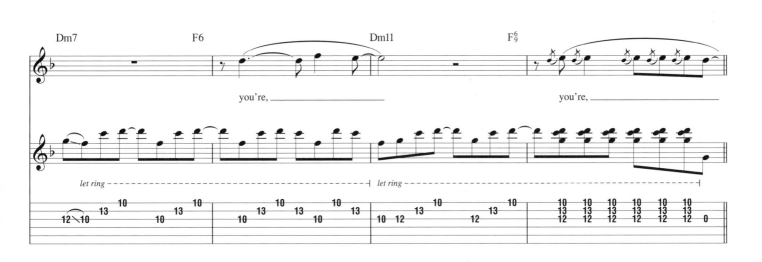

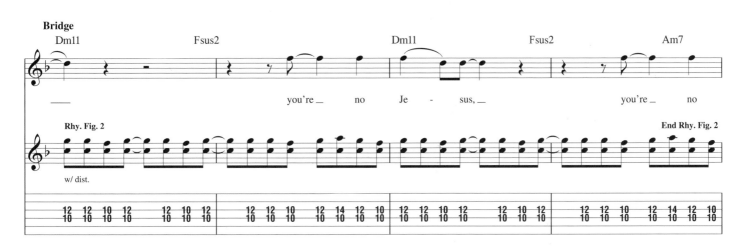

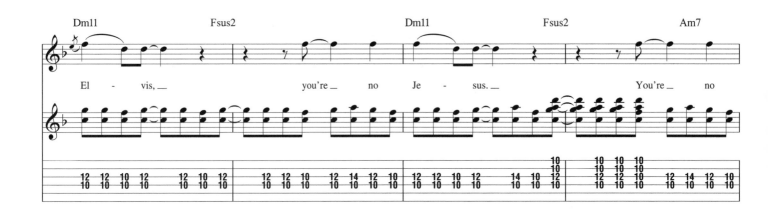

Gtrs. 1 & 4: w/ Rhy. Fig. 2 (2 times)

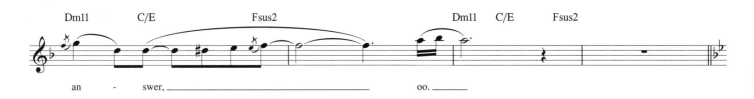

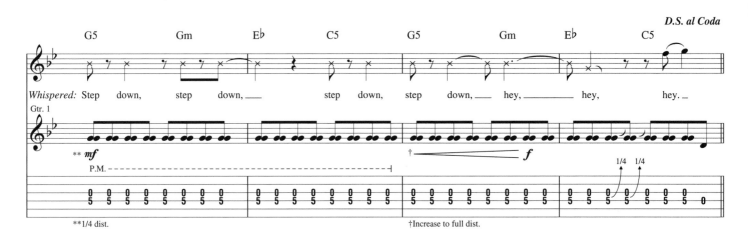

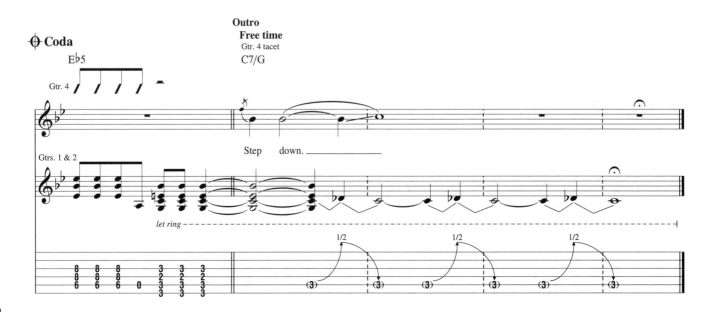

**Outro**
**Free time**
Gtr. 4 tacet

# Ocean Avenue

**Words and Music by Ryan Key, Sean Mackin, Ben Harper and Longineu Parsons**

Drop D tuning:
(low to high) D-A-D-G-B-E

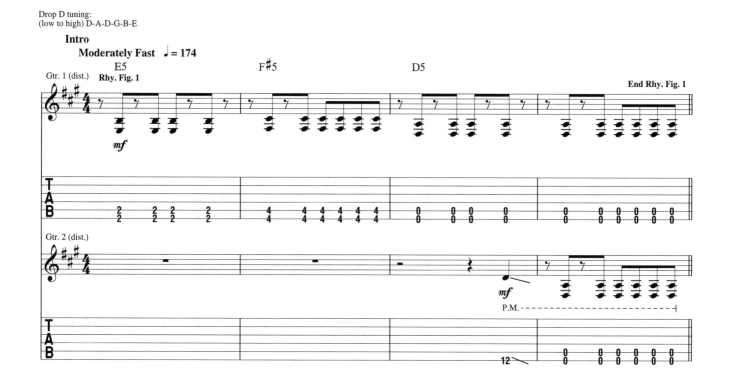

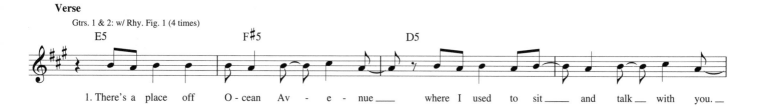

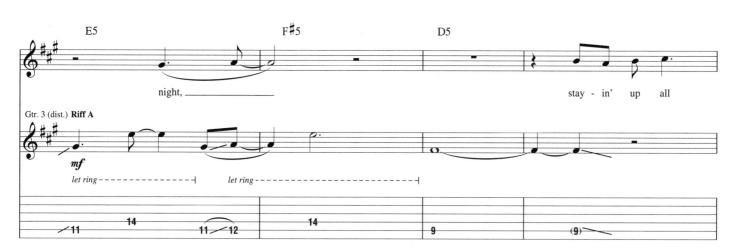

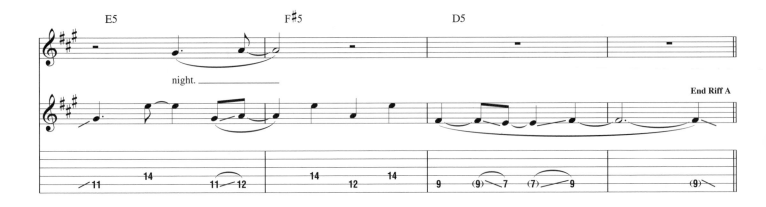

night. _____

End Riff A

**Verse**
Gtrs. 1 & 2: w/ Rhy. Fig. 1 (3 times)
Gtr. 3 tacet

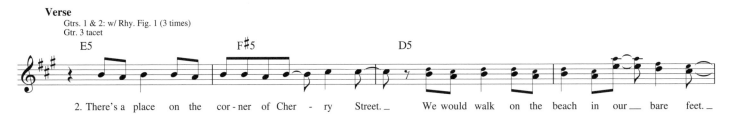

2. There's a place on the cor-ner of Cher-ry Street. _ We would walk on the beach in our _ bare feet. _

_ We were both eight-een and it felt _ so right, _ sleep-in' all

Gtr. 3: w/ Riff A

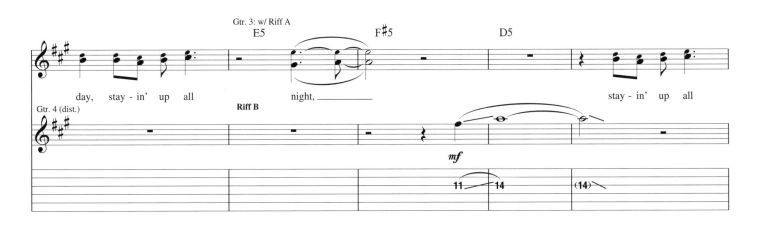

day, stay-in' up all night, _ stay-in' up all

Gtr. 4 (dist.)
**Riff B**

*mf*

E5 F#5 D5

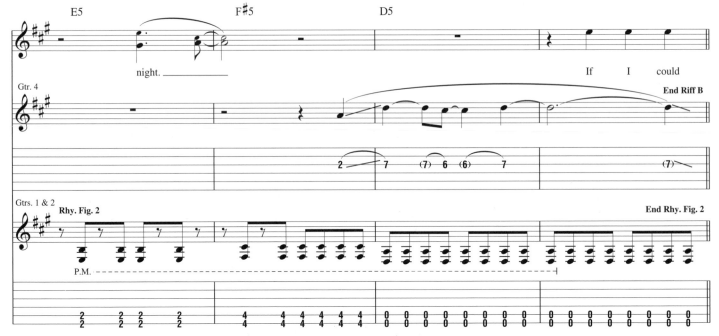

night. _____

If I could

Gtr. 4

End Riff B

Gtrs. 1 & 2
**Rhy. Fig. 2**

End Rhy. Fig. 2

P.M. ------------------------

**Chorus**

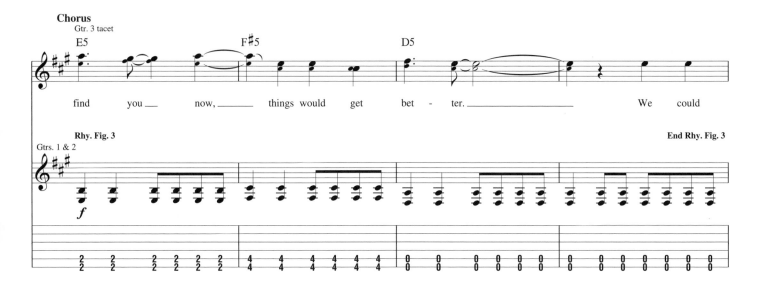

find you ___ now, ___ things would get bet - ter. ___ We could

leave this ___ town ___ and run for - ev - er. ___ Let your

waves crash ___ down ___ on me and take me ___ a - way, ___ yeah, ___ yeah.

**Interlude**

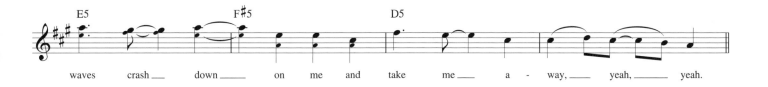

**Verse**

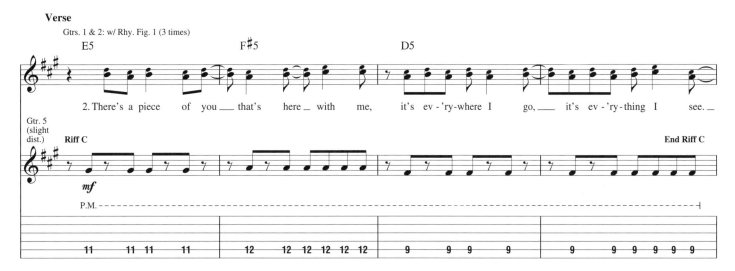

2. There's a piece of you ___ that's here ___ with me, it's ev-'ry-where I go, it's ev-'ry-thing I see.

Gtr. 5: w/ Riff C

When I sleep, I dream and it gets me by. I can make be-lieve that you're here

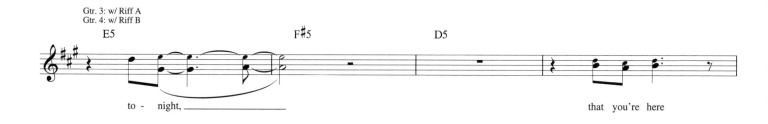

Gtr. 3: w/ Riff A
Gtr. 4: w/ Riff B

to - night, that you're here

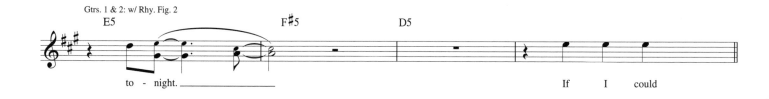

Gtrs. 1 & 2: w/ Rhy. Fig. 2

to - night. If I could

### Chorus
Gtrs. 1 & 2: w/ Rhy. Fig. 3 (4 times)

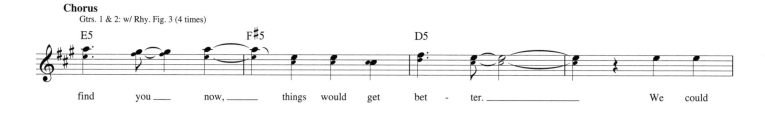

find you now, things would get bet - ter. We could

leave this town and run for - ev - er. I know some -

where, some - how, we'll be to - geth - er. Let your

waves crash down on me and take me a - way, yeah.

**Interlude**

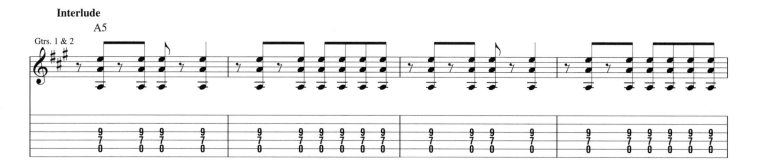

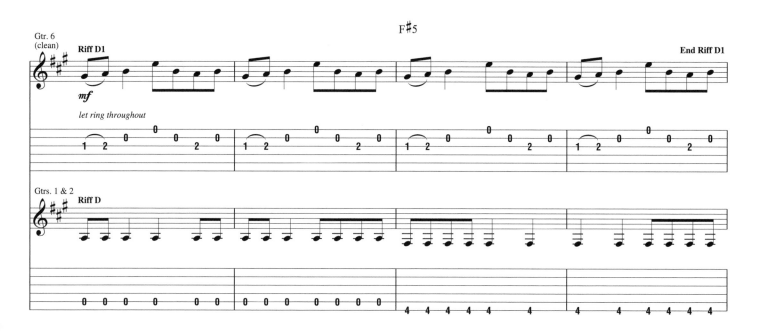

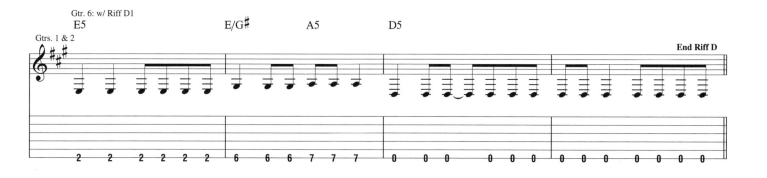

**Bridge**

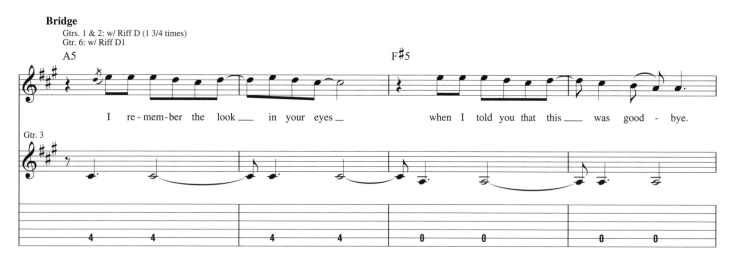

I re-mem-ber the look ___ in your eyes ___ when I told you that this ___ was good - bye.

**Chorus**
Gtr. 1: w/ Rhy. Fig. 3
Gtr. 3 tacet

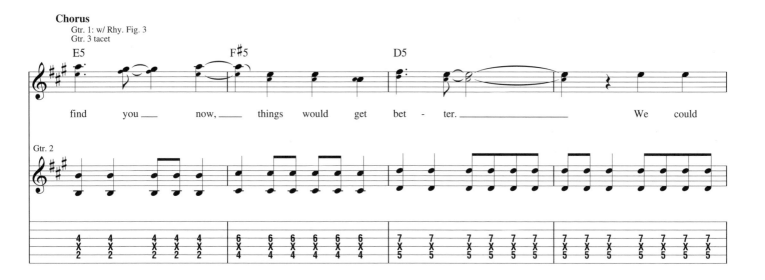

find you ___ now, ___ things would get bet - ter. ___ We could

leave this ___ town ___ and run for - ev - er. ___ I know some -

Gtr. 1: w/ Rhy Fig. 3 (2 times)

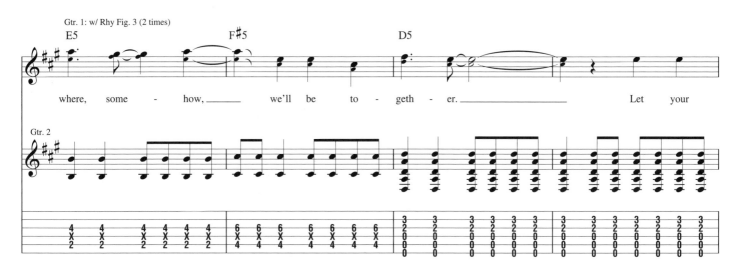

where, some - how, ___ we'll be to - geth - er. ___ Let your

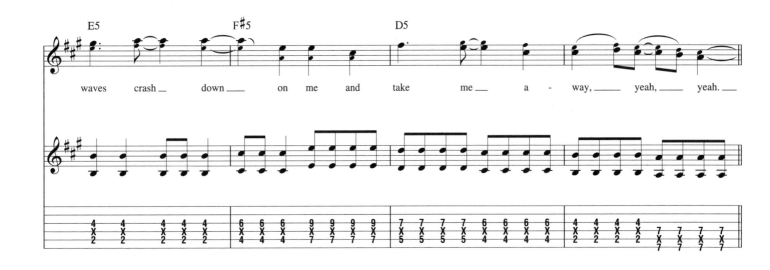

waves crash down on me and take me a - way, yeah, yeah.

**Outro**

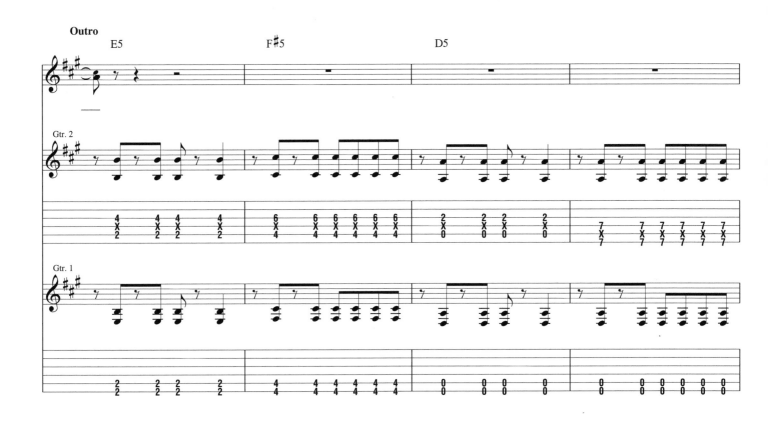

Gtr. 2

Gtr. 1

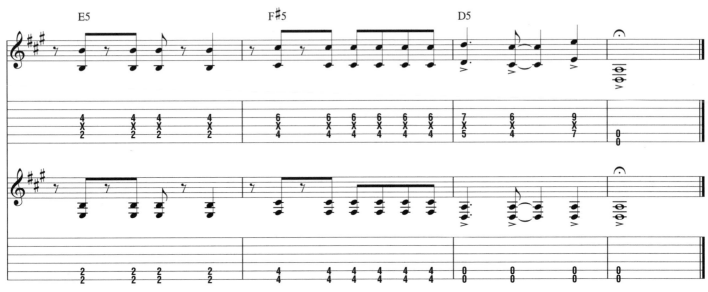

# The Outsider

**Words and Music by Maynard James Keenan and Billy Howerdel**

Tune down 1 1/2 steps:
(low to high) C#-F#-B-E-G#-C#

**Intro**

**Moderately slow** ♩ = 57

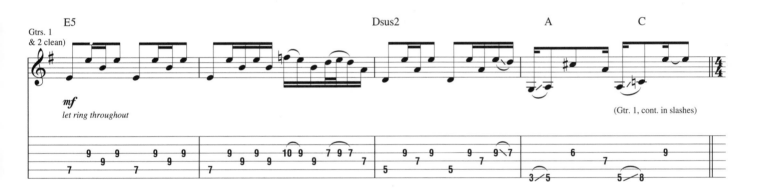

*Chord symbols reflect implied harmony.

**Verse**

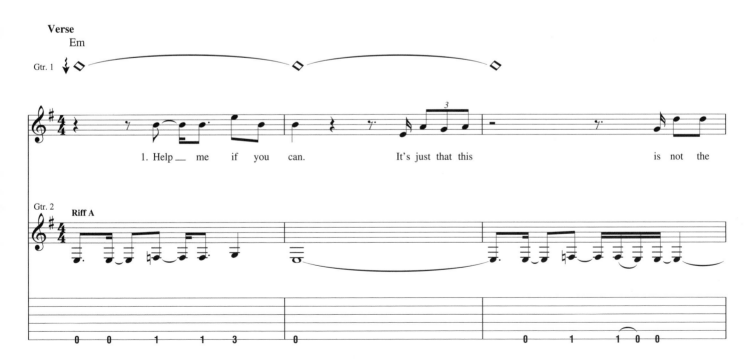

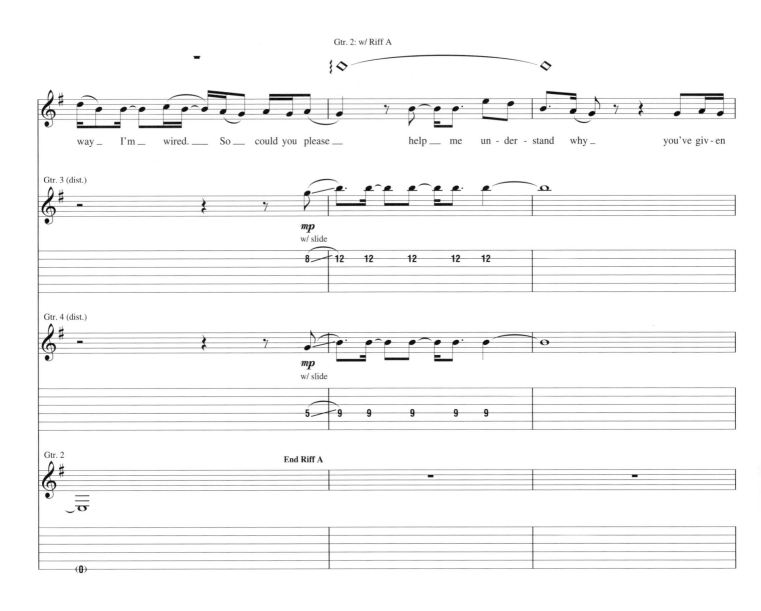

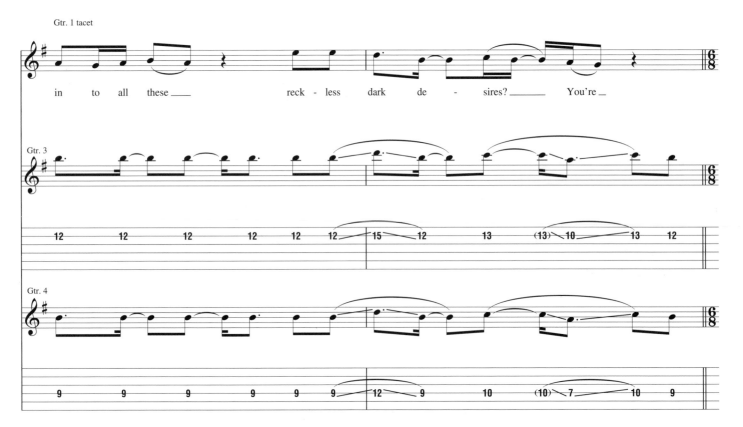

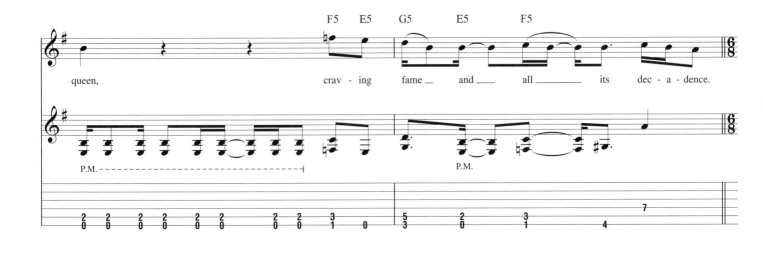

queen, crav - ing fame _ and _ all _____ its dec - a - dence.

**Pre-Chorus**

Gtrs. 3 & 4: w/ Riffs B & B1
Gtr. 5: w/ Riff B2 (2 times)

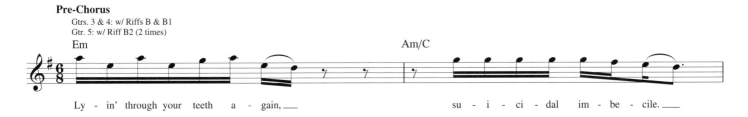

Ly - in' through your teeth a - gain, __ su - i - ci - dal im - be - cile. __

Think a - bout it, put it on the fault - line. What-'ll it take to get it through to you, pre - cious?

Mm, o - ver this. Why you wan - na throw it a - way like this? Such a mess. I don't wan - na watch you. __

**Chorus**

Dis - con - nect and __ self de - struct one __ bul - let __ at __ a __

88

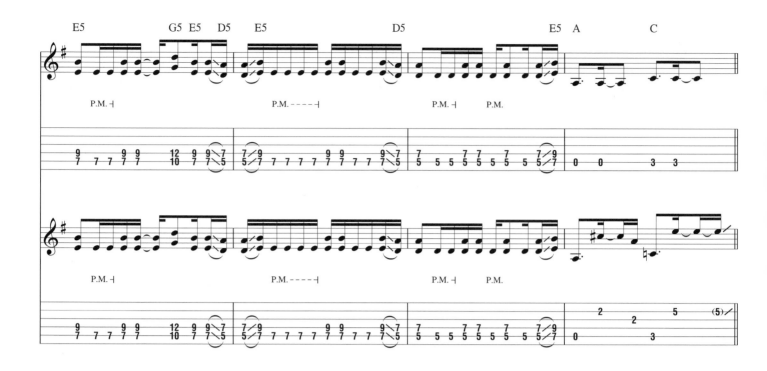

## Outro-Chorus

Dis - con - nect and __ self de - struct one __ bul - let __ at a __ time.

Gtrs. 5 & 6

8va-- loco

Harm. -|

Pitch: B   E

What's your __ hur - ry? __ Ev - 'ry - one __ will __ have his __ day to __ die.

P.M. ------|

If you __ choose to __ pull the __ trig- ger, should your __ dra - ma __ prove sin - cere,

do it __ some - where __ far a - way from __ here.

# Running Blind

**Words and Music by Sully Erna**

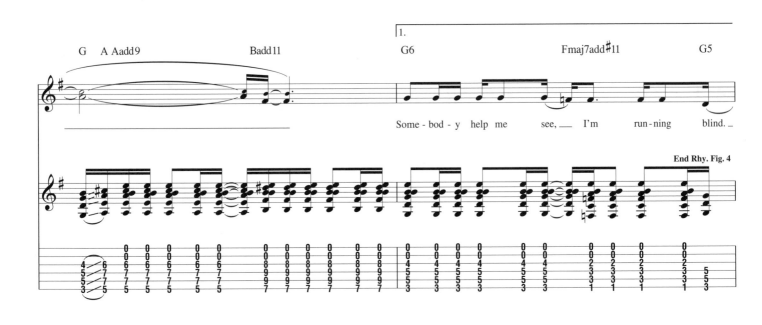

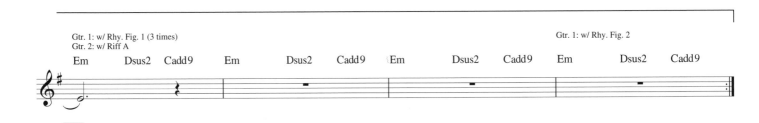

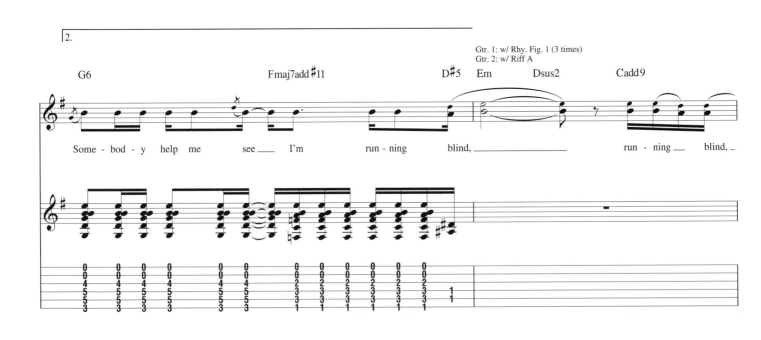

**Guitar Solo**

Gtr. 1: w/ Rhy. Fig. 1 (4 times)

Gtr. 1: w/ Rhy. Fig. 4

**Interlude**

Gtr. 1: w/ Rhy. Fig. 1 (3 times)          Gtr. 3 tacet                                        Gtr. 1: w/ Rhy. Fig. 2
Gtr. 2: w/ Riff A

**Verse**

Gtr. 1: w/ Rhy. Fig. 1 (4 times)

3. I can't find the an - swers. __          I've been crawl - ing on __ my knees __

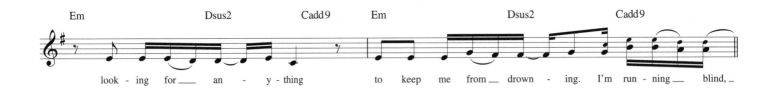

look - ing for __ an - y - thing to keep me from __ drown - ing. I'm run - ning __ blind,

**Outro**

Gtr.. 1: w/ Rhy. Fig. 1 (7 times)

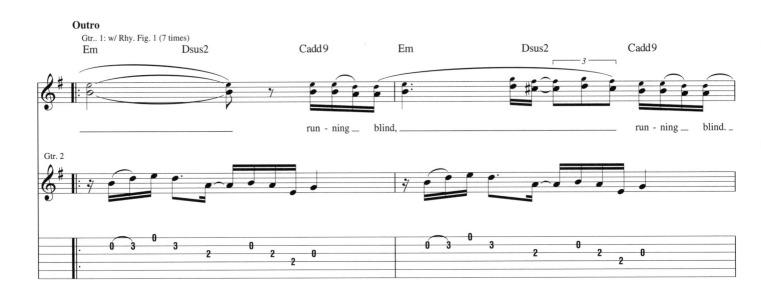

run - ning __ blind, _____ run - ning __ blind. __

Gtr. 2

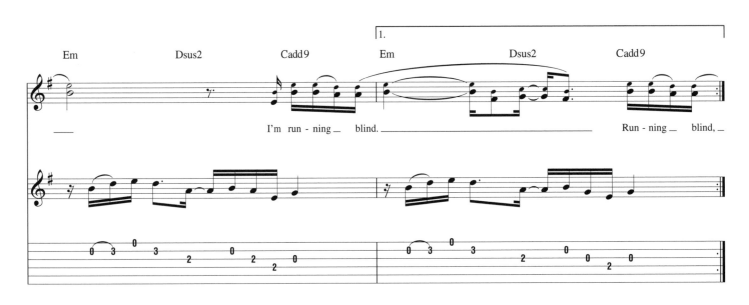

I'm run - ning __ blind. _____ Run - ning __ blind, __

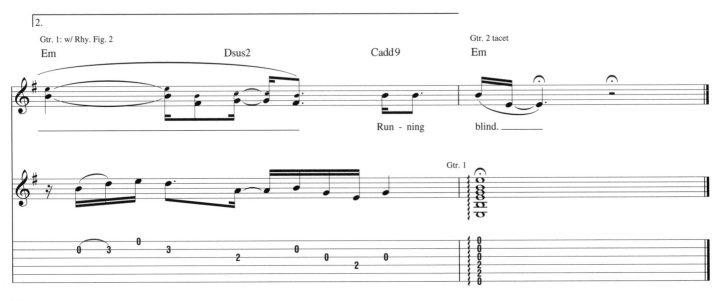

Gtr. 1: w/ Rhy. Fig. 2

Run - ning          blind. __

# This Love

**Words and Music by Adam Levine and Jesse Carmichael**

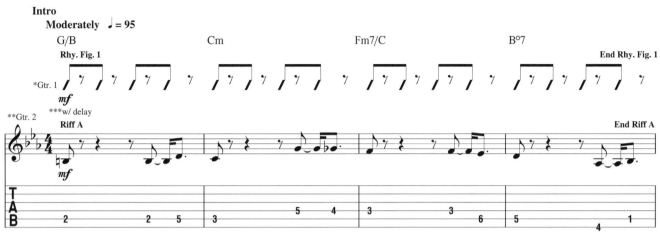

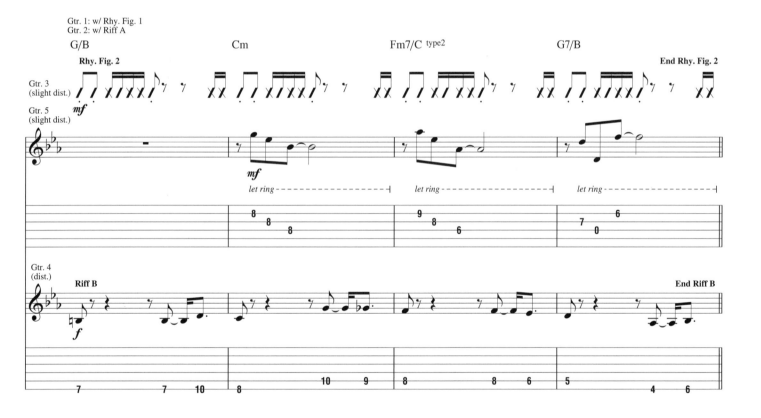

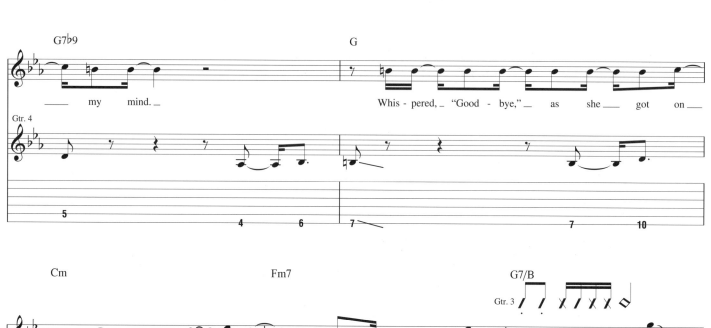

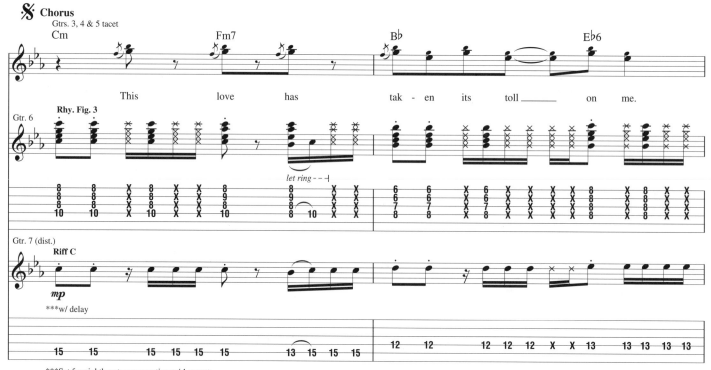

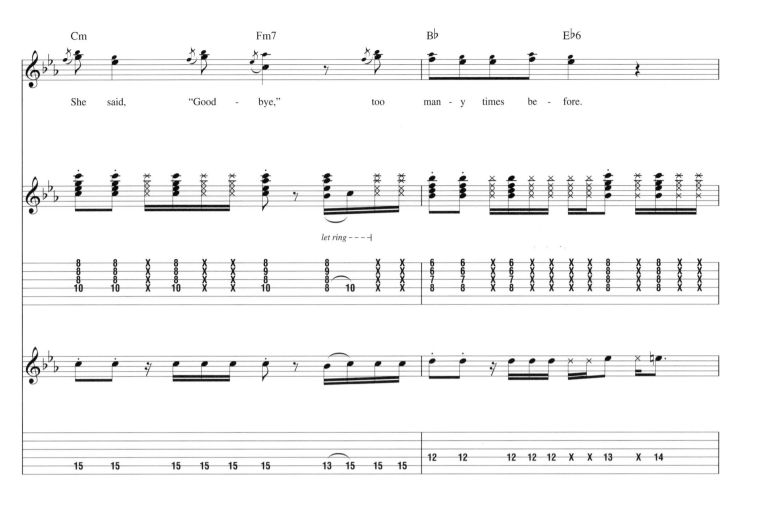

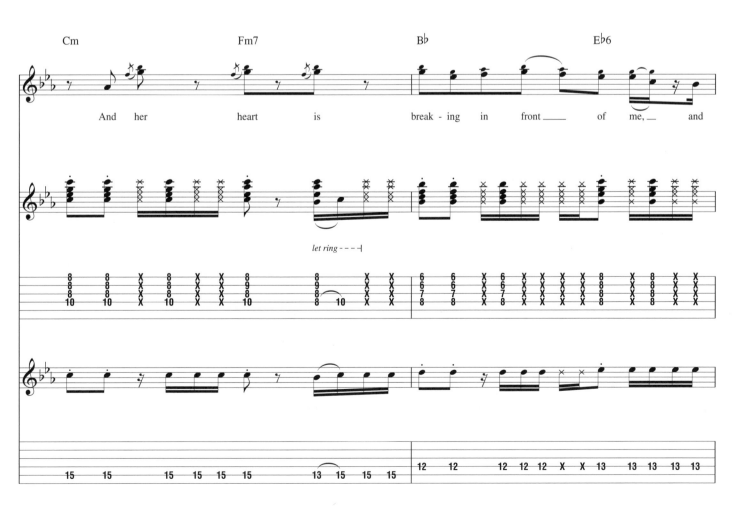

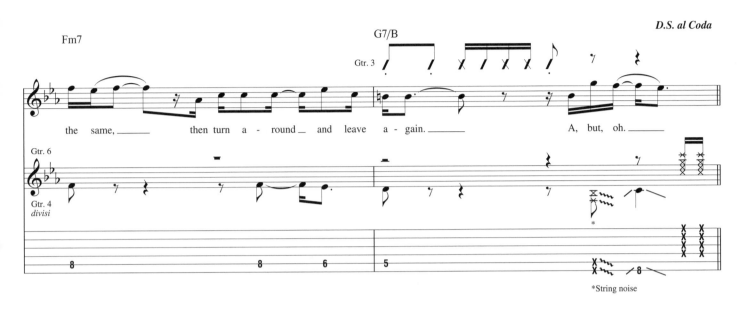

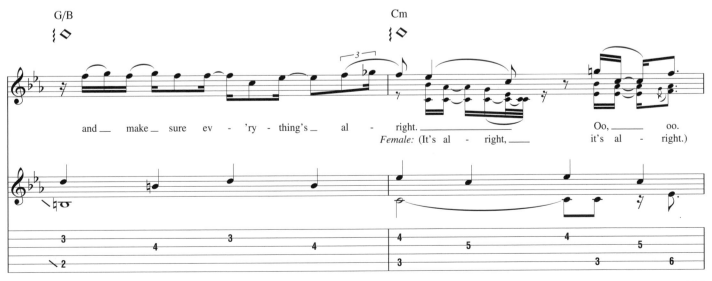

My pres - sure on your hips, ah, sink - ing my fin - ger - tips in - to

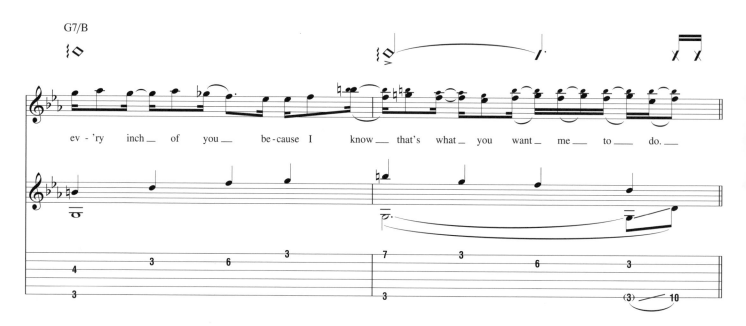

ev - 'ry inch of you be - cause I know that's what you want me to do.

**Outro-Chorus**
Gtr. 6: w/ Rhy. Fig. 3 (till fade)
Gtr. 7: w/ Riff C
Gtr. 9 tacet

This love has tak - en its toll on me.

She said, "Good - bye," too man - y times be - fore. Her heart is

break - ing in front of me, and I have no choice 'cause

**102**

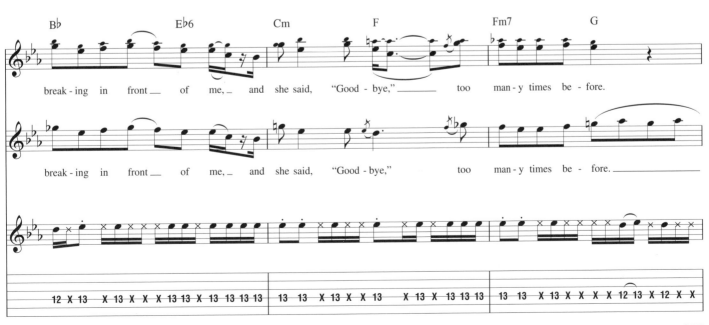

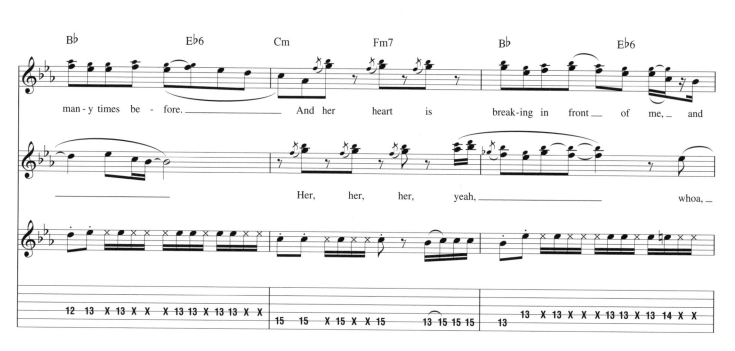

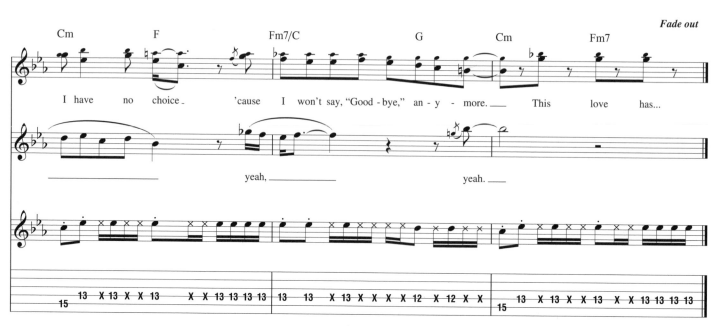

# What You Are

### Lyrics by Chris Cornell
### Music written and arranged by Audioslave

Gtr. 1

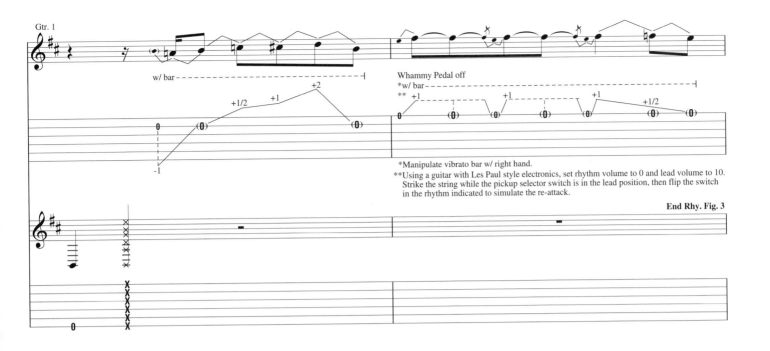

*Manipulate vibrato bar w/ right hand.
**Using a guitar with Les Paul style electronics, set rhythm volume to 0 and lead volume to 10.
  Strike the string while the pickup selector switch is in the lead position, then flip the switch
  in the rhythm indicated to simulate the re-attack.

**End Rhy. Fig. 3**

Gtr. 2: w/ Rhy. Fig. 3

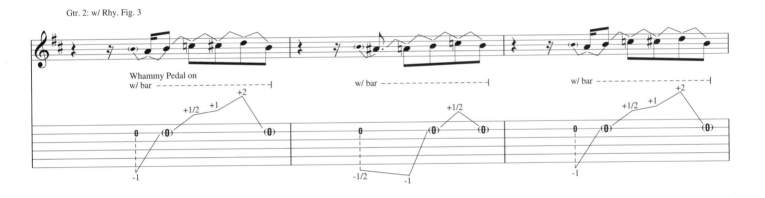

**Bridge**
N.C.

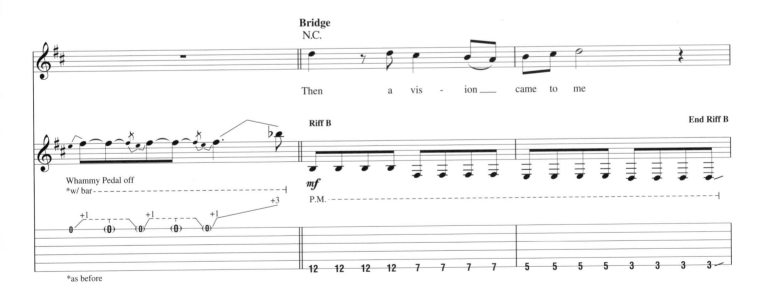

Then     a   vis - ion ___ came   to   me

**Riff B**                                                                  **End Riff B**

*as before

Gtr. 1: w/ Riff B (2 1/2 times)

when          you ___          came  a - long. ___          I     gave ___  you ___

107

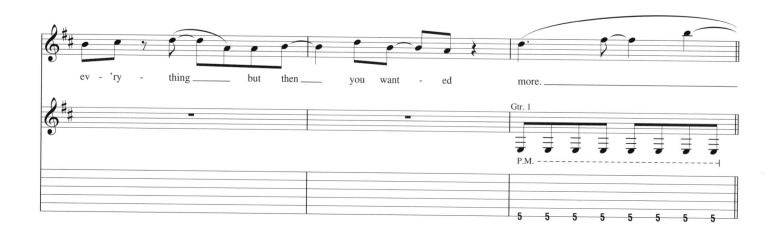

ev - 'ry - thing _____ but then _____ you want - ed more. _____

## Chorus

Gtrs. 1 & 2: w/ Rhy. Fig. 1 (3 times)

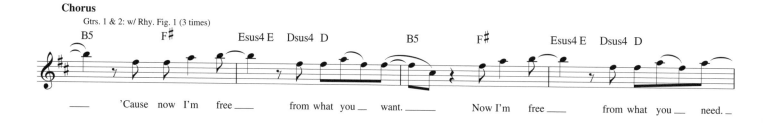

| B5 | | F# | | Esus4 | E | Dsus4 | D | | B5 | | F# | | Esus4 | E | Dsus4 | D |

_____ 'Cause now I'm free _____ from what you __ want. _____ Now I'm free _____ from what you __ need.

Gtrs. 1 & 2: w/ Rhy. Fig. 2 (1st meas., 2 times)

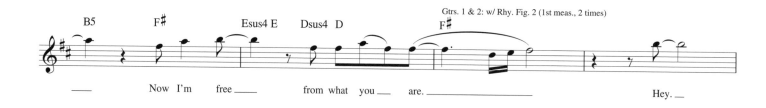

| B5 | | F# | | Esus4 | E | | Dsus4 | D | | F# |

_____ Now I'm free _____ from what you __ are. _____ Hey. __

Gtrs. 1 & 2: w/ Rhy. Fig. 1 (3 times)

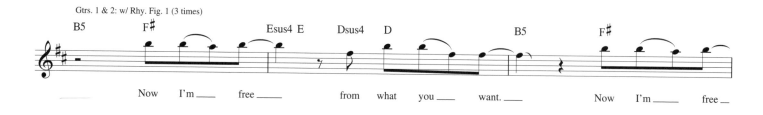

| B5 | | F# | | Esus4 | E | | Dsus4 | D | | B5 | | F# |

_____ Now I'm __ free _____ from what you ___ want. _____ Now I'm ___ free __

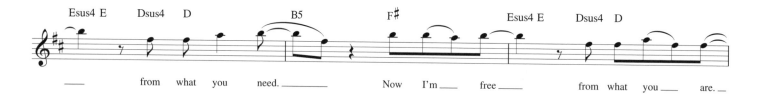

| Esus4 | E | | Dsus4 | D | | B5 | | F# | | Esus4 | E | Dsus4 | D |

_____ from what you __ need. _____ Now I'm ___ free _____ from what you ___ are. __

| F# | | | N.C. |

Gtrs. 1 & 2

# Guitar Notation Legend

Guitar Music can be notated three different ways: on a *musical staff*, in *tablature*, and in *rhythm slashes*.

**RHYTHM SLASHES** are written above the staff. Strum chords in the rhythm indicated. Use the chord diagrams found at the top of the first page of the transcription for the appropriate chord voicings. Round noteheads indicate single notes.

**THE MUSICAL STAFF** shows pitches and rhythms and is divided by bar lines into measures. Pitches are named after the first seven letters of the alphabet.

**TABLATURE** graphically represents the guitar fingerboard. Each horizontal line represents a a string, and each number represents a fret.

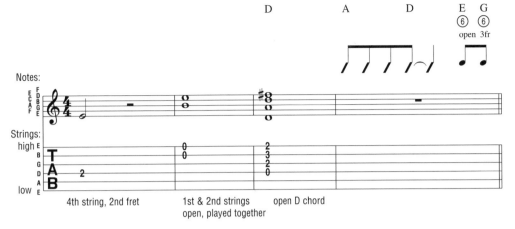

4th string, 2nd fret

1st & 2nd strings open, played together

open D chord

# Definitions for Special Guitar Notation

**HALF-STEP BEND:** Strike the note and bend up 1/2 step.

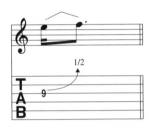

**WHOLE-STEP BEND:** Strike the note and bend up one step.

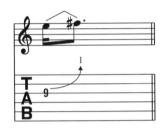

**GRACE NOTE BEND:** Strike the note and immediately bend up as indicated.

**SLIGHT (MICROTONE) BEND:** Strike the note and bend up 1/4 step.

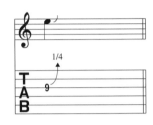

**BEND AND RELEASE:** Strike the note and bend up as indicated, then release back to the original note. Only the first note is struck.

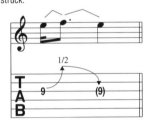

**PRE-BEND:** Bend the note as indicated, then strike it.

**PRE-BEND AND RELEASE:** Bend the note as indicated. Strike it and release the bend back to the original note.

**UNISON BEND:** Strike the two notes simultaneously and bend the lower note up to the pitch of the higher.

**VIBRATO:** The string is vibrated by rapidly bending and releasing the note with the fretting hand.

**WIDE VIBRATO:** The pitch is varied to a greater degree by vibrating with the fretting hand.

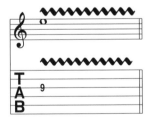

**HAMMER-ON:** Strike the first (lower) note with one finger, then sound the higher note (on the same string) with another finger by fretting it without picking.

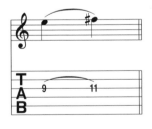

**PULL-OFF:** Place both fingers on the notes to be sounded. Strike the first note and without picking, pull the finger off to sound the second (lower) note.

**LEGATO SLIDE:** Strike the first note and then slide the same fret-hand finger up or down to the second note. The second note is not struck.

**SHIFT SLIDE:** Same as legato slide, except the second note is struck.

**TRILL:** Very rapidly alternate between the notes indicated by continuously hammering on and pulling off.

**TAPPING:** Hammer ("tap") the fret indicated with the pick-hand index or middle finger and pull off to the note fretted by the fret hand.

**NATURAL HARMONIC:** Strike the note while the fret-hand lightly touches the string directly over the fret indicated.

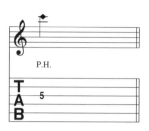

**PINCH HARMONIC:** The note is fretted normally and a harmonic is produced by adding the edge of the thumb or the tip of the index finger of the pick hand to the normal pick attack.

**HARP HARMONIC:** The note is fretted normally and a harmonic is produced by gently resting the pick hand's index finger directly above the indicated fret (in parentheses) while the pick hand's thumb or pick assists by plucking the appropriate string.

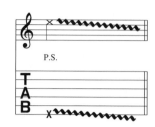

**PICK SCRAPE:** The edge of the pick is rubbed down (or up) the string, producing a scratchy sound.

**MUFFLED STRINGS:** A percussive sound is produced by laying the fret hand across the string(s) without depressing, and striking them with the pick hand.

**PALM MUTING:** The note is partially muted by the pick hand lightly touching the string(s) just before the bridge.

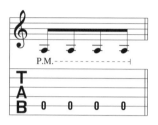

**RAKE:** Drag the pick across the strings indicated with a single motion.

**TREMOLO PICKING:** The note is picked as rapidly and continuously as possible.

**ARPEGGIATE:** Play the notes of the chord indicated by quickly rolling them from bottom to top.

**VIBRATO BAR DIVE AND RETURN:** The pitch of the note or chord is dropped a specified number of steps (in rhythm) then returned to the original pitch.

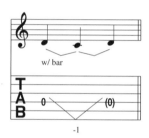

**VIBRATO BAR SCOOP:** Depress the bar just before striking the note, then quickly release the bar.

**VIBRATO BAR DIP:** Strike the note and then immediately drop a specified number of steps, then release back to the original pitch.

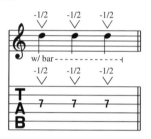

# Additional Musical Definitions

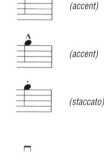

| | | |
|---|---|---|
| | (accent) | • Accentuate note (play it louder) |
| | (accent) | • Accentuate note with great intensity |
| | (staccato) | • Play the note short |
| ⊓ | | • Downstroke |
| V | | • Upstroke |

**D.S. al Coda**
• Go back to the sign ( 𝄋 ), then play until the measure marked "*To Coda*," then skip to the section labelled "**Coda**."

**D.C. al Fine**
• Go back to the beginning of the song and play until the measure marked "*Fine*" (end).

**Rhy. Fig.**
• Label used to recall a recurring accompaniment pattern (usually chordal).

**Riff**
• Label used to recall composed, melodic lines (usually single notes) which recur.

**Fill**
• Label used to identify a brief melodic figure which is to be inserted into the arrangement.

**Rhy. Fill**
• A chordal version of a Fill.

**tacet**
• Instrument is silent (drops out).

• Repeat measures between signs.

• When a repeated section has different endings, play the first ending only the first time and the second ending only the second time.

**NOTE:** Tablature numbers in parentheses mean:
1. The note is being sustained over a system (note in standard notation is tied), or
2. The note is sustained, but a new articulation (such as a hammer-on, pull-off, slide or vibrato begins), or
3. The note is a barely audible "ghost" note (note in standard notation is also in parentheses).

# RECORDED VERSIONS

## The Best Note-For-Note Transcriptions Available

**ALL BOOKS INCLUDE TABLATURE**

# GUITAR PLAY-ALONG

This series will help you play your favorite songs quickly and easily. Just follow the tab and listen to the CD to hear how the guitar should sound, and then play along using the separate backing tracks. Mac or PC users can also slow down the tempo by using the CD in their computer. The melody and lyrics are also included in the book so that you can sing or simply follow along.

**INCLUDES TAB**

### VOL. 1 – ROCK GUITAR  00699570 / $12.95
Day Tripper • Message in a Bottle • Refugee • Shattered • Sunshine of Your Love • Takin' Care of Business • Tush • Walk This Way.

### VOL. 2 – ACOUSTIC  00699569 / $12.95
Angie • Behind Blue Eyes • Best of My Love • Blackbird • Dust in the Wind • Layla • Night Moves • Yesterday.

### VOL. 3 – HARD ROCK  00699573 / $14.95
Crazy Train • Iron Man • Living After Midnight • Rock You Like a Hurricane • Round and Round • Smoke on the Water • Sweet Child O' Mine • You Really Got Me.

### VOL. 4 – POP/ROCK  00699571 / $12.95
Breakdown • Crazy Little Thing Called Love • Hit Me with Your Best Shot • I Want You to Want Me • Lights • R.O.C.K. in the U.S.A. (A Salute to 60's Rock) • Summer of '69 • What I Like About You.

### VOL. 5 – MODERN ROCK  00699574 / $12.95
Aerials • Alive • Bother • Chop Suey! • Control • Last Resort • Take a Look Around (Theme from "M:I-2") • Wish You Were Here.

### VOL. 6 – '90S ROCK  00699572 / $12.95
Are You Gonna Go My Way • Come Out and Play • I'll Stick Around • Know Your Enemy • Man in the Box • Outshined • Smells Like Teen Spirit • Under the Bridge.

### VOL. 7 – BLUES GUITAR  00699575 / $12.95
All Your Love (I Miss Loving) • Born Under a Bad Sign • Hide Away • I'm Tore Down • I'm Your Hoochie Coochie Man • Pride and Joy • Sweet Home Chicago • The Thrill Is Gone.

### VOL. 8 – ROCK  00699585 / $12.95
All Right Now • Black Magic Woman • Get Back • Hey Joe • Layla • Love Me Two Times • Won't Get Fooled Again • You Really Got Me.

### VOL. 9 – PUNK ROCK  00699576 / $12.95
All the Small Things • Fat Lip • Flavor of the Weak • I Feel So • Lifestyles of the Rich and Famous • (So) Tired of Waiting for You • Say It Ain't So • Self Esteem.

### VOL. 10 – ACOUSTIC  00699586 / $12.95
Here Comes the Sun • Landslide • The Magic Bus • Norwegian Wood (This Bird Has Flown) • Pink Houses • Space Oddity • Tangled Up in Blue • Tears in Heaven.

### VOL. 11 – EARLY ROCK  00699579 / $12.95
Fun, Fun, Fun • Hound Dog • Louie, Louie • No Particular Place to Go • Oh, Pretty Woman • Rock Around the Clock • Under the Boardwalk • Wild Thing.

### VOL. 12 – POP/ROCK  00699587 / $12.95
867-5309/Jenny • Every Breath You Take • Money for Nothing • Rebel, Rebel • Run to You • Ticket to Ride • Wonderful Tonight • You Give Love a Bad Name.

### VOL. 13 – FOLK ROCK  00699581 / $12.95
Annie's Song • Leaving on a Jet Plane • Suite: Judy Blue Eyes • This Land Is Your Land • Time in a Bottle • Turn! Turn! Turn! (To Everything There Is a Season) • You've Got a Friend • You've Got to Hide Your Love Away.

### VOL. 14 – BLUES ROCK  00699582 / $14.95
Blue on Black • Crossfire • Cross Road Blues (Crossroads) • The House Is Rockin' • La Grange • Move It on Over • Roadhouse Blues • Statesboro Blues.

### VOL. 15 – R&B  00699583 / $12.95
Ain't Too Proud to Beg • Brick House • Get Ready • I Can't Help Myself (Sugar Pie, Honey Bunch) • I Got You (I Feel Good) • I Heard It Through the Grapevine • My Girl • Shining Star.

### VOL. 16 – JAZZ  00699584 / $12.95
All Blues • Bluesette • Footprints • How Insensitive (Insensatez) • Misty • Satin Doll • Stella by Starlight • Tenor Madness.

### VOL. 17 – COUNTRY  00699588 / $12.95
Amie • Boot Scootin' Boogie • Chattahoochee • Folsom Prison Blues • Friends in Low Places • Forever and Ever, Amen • T-R-O-U-B-L-E • Workin' Man Blues.

### VOL. 18 – ACOUSTIC ROCK  00699577 / $14.95
About a Girl • Breaking the Girl • Drive • Iris • More Than Words • Patience • Silent Lucidity • 3 AM.

### VOL. 19 – SOUL  00699578 / $12.95
Get Up (I Feel Like Being) a Sex Machine • Green Onions • In the Midnight Hour • Knock on Wood • Mustang Sally • Respect • (Sittin' On) the Dock of the Bay • Soul Man.

### VOL. 20 – ROCKABILLY  00699580 / $12.95
Be-Bop-A-Lula • Blue Suede Shoes • Hello Mary Lou • Little Sister • Mystery Train • Rock This Town • Stray Cat Strut • That'll Be the Day.

### VOL. 21 – YULETIDE  00699602 / $12.95
Angels We Have Heard on High • Away in a Manger • Deck the Hall • The First Noel • Go, Tell It on the Mountain • Jingle Bells • Joy to the World • O Little Town of Bethlehem.

### VOL. 22 – CHRISTMAS  00699600 / $12.95
The Christmas Song (Chestnuts Roasting on an Open Fire) • Frosty the Snow Man • Happy Xmas (War Is Over) • Here Comes Santa Claus (Right Down Santa Claus Lane) • Jingle-Bell Rock • Merry Christmas, Darling • Rudolph the Red-Nosed Reindeer • Silver Bells.

### VOL. 23 – SURF  00699635 / $12.95
Let's Go Trippin' • Out of Limits • Penetration • Pipeline • Surf City • Surfin' U.S.A. • Walk Don't Run • The Wedge.

### VOL. 24 – ERIC CLAPTON  00699649 / $14.95
Badge • Bell Bottom Blues • Change the World • Cocaine • Key to the Highway • Lay Down Sally • White Room • Wonderful Tonight.

### VOL. 25 – LENNON AND MCCARTNEY  00699642 / $14.95
Back in the U.S.S.R. • Drive My Car • Get Back • A Hard Day's Night • I Feel Fine • Paperback Writer • Revolution • Ticket to Ride.

### VOL. 26 – ELVIS PRESLEY  00699643 / $14.95
All Shook Up • Blue Suede Shoes • Don't Be Cruel (To a Heart That's True) • Heartbreak Hotel • Hound Dog • Jailhouse Rock • Little Sister • Mystery Train.

### VOL. 27 – DAVID LEE ROTH  00699645 / $14.95
Ain't Talkin' 'Bout Love • Dance the Night Away • Just Like Paradise • A Lil' Ain't Enough • Panama • Runnin' with the Devil • Unchained • Yankee Rose.

### VOL. 28 – GREG KOCH  00699646 / $14.95
Chief's Blues • Death of a Bassman • Dylan the Villain • The Grip • Holy Grail • Spank It • Tonus Diabolicus • Zoiks.

### VOL. 29 – BOB SEGER  00699647 / $14.95
Against the Wind • Betty Lou's Gettin' Out Tonight • Hollywood Nights • Mainstreet • Night Moves • Old Time Rock & Roll • Rock and Roll Never Forgets • Still the Same.

### VOL. 30 – KISS  00699644 / $14.95
Cold Gin • Detroit Rock City • Deuce • Firehouse • Heaven's on Fire • Love Gun • Rock and Roll All Nite • Shock Me.

### VOL. 31 – CHRISTMAS HITS  00699652 / $12.95
Blue Christmas • Do You Hear What I Hear • Happy Holiday • I Saw Mommy Kissing Santa Claus • I'll Be Home for Christmas • Let It Snow! Let It Snow! Let It Snow! • Little Saint Nick • Snowfall.

*Prices, contents, and availability subject to change without notice.*

FOR MORE INFORMATION, SEE YOUR LOCAL MUSIC DEALER, OR WRITE TO:

HAL•LEONARD
CORPORATION
7777 W. BLUEMOUND RD. P.O. BOX 13819 MILWAUKEE, WI 5321

**Visit Hal Leonard online at www.halleonard**